THE WORLD'S BEST

SPICY

FOOD

WHERE TO FIND IT
& HOW TO MAKE IT

y planet
food

CONTENTS

INTRODUCTION

BY TOM PARKER BOWLES

It started with a drop, beguilingly red and devilishly scented, poured from a small, elegant bottle onto the back of my hand.

'Go on, try it,' my sister implored, her eyes glittering with glee. 'All the grown ups drink the stuff. How dangerous can it be?' So I closed my eyes tight, and plunged my tongue into the unknown. The first taste was sharp but not unpleasant, like the vinegar that we splashed on our chips. I smiled, and sighed with relief. Much ado about nothing. And then it hit, a fierce, brutally burning sensation that started in my mouth before spreading, like a raging forest fire, across my lips and down into my throat.

My eyes brimmed with tears. I tried to scream but to no avail. I'd never felt pain like this. It was worse than stinging nettles and grazed knees and the slap of a cold football on rain-drenched flesh. I fell to the floor, clutching my belly, convinced that this damned liquid was noxious poison, the killer of small boys.

Then, as suddenly as it had begun, the agony abated. I opened my eyes and looked about. The light seemed brighter, every colour more vivid. Sure, my tongue still throbbed and my lips smarted. But my whole body was enveloped in a warm glow. My sister was sheet-white and trembling, convinced she was the architect of her brother's demise. I, though, was in love. One drop of Tabasco sauce, and I've never looked back since.

Soon, I was splashing this beautiful Louisiana hot sauce over everything that was put before me, from toast and egg to steak and shepherd's pie. And this was just the start: Tabasco was the gateway drug of an addiction that would take over my life. Curries followed, each more potent than the next, madras first, then the great leap to vindaloo. I began to cook with chillies, moving quickly from dull long green things to the fruity insanity of the Scotch bonnet. Before long, I was a subscriber to Chile Pepper magazine, scouring the streets for my next spicy hit.

Visits to Thailand followed, som toms with enough bird's-eye punch to floor a rampaging bull elephant, let alone a rather pasty Brit. Tom yam gungs, fragrant with heat and fish sauce, nam phrik pla flowing like monsoon-bloated rivers. I just couldn't get enough: it was pain, sure, but exquisite pleasure too. There were dhals eaten in India at roadside shops, little more than ten pence a portion, but thick with great lengths of

dried Kashmiri chilli. And Indonesian sambals, in every hue and pong.

I visited hot-sauce shows in Albuquerque, New Mexico: entire conference centres devoted to fiery foods. And fell in love with the chile con carne of Texas, plus the entire cuisine of Mexico, from birrias and ceviches to tortillas and tostadas. I huffed and puffed my way through incendiary, but impossibly crisp, hot chicken at Prince's in Nashville, Tennessee, breakfast burritos smothered with green chile in Santa Fe, New Mexico. And bought Caribbean hot sauces bottled in old Lucozade bottles from roadside stalls in Antigua. Then there's kimchi in Korea, harissa-spiked couscous, Sichuan chilli hotpots and everything in between.

I love the chilli more than any other fruit, pretty much more than any ingredient there is. It's not all about heat, rather, huge complexities of flavour and texture and joy. The smoky heft of a chipotle chilli, the verdant tang of a fresh jalapeno. But the reason why the chilli pepper is so damned addictive lies in its active ingredient, capsaicin, a nasty little irritant alkaloid. The hotter the chilli, the more of this chemical it contains, hitting the taste buds hard, sending them reeling in pain. So the body reacts, and sends in the Special Forces (better known as endorphins). That's why the agony is followed by that blissful state of dreamy joy. As these endorphins flood the system, putting out the fires, we experience a truly natural 'high'.

But this book is not about chillies alone, rather 'spicy' food in its every guise. The pungent, nose-clearing honk of wasabi, mustard and horseradish; pepper's pep (black, white, pink and Sichuan) and paprika's punch; the warming allure of cinnamon and mace, the bracing crunch of piccalilli. These are dishes to make the taste buds punch the air with elation, flavours that kickstart the palate and infuse every sense with joy.

As you'd expect, there are a huge number of dishes from Thailand, India and Mexico, the three great chilli cuisines, alongside Sichuan Chinese and Korean too. But we also feast upon herrings from Norway,

Turkish kebabs, Czech sausages and African chicken. Trindadian souse sits alongside Hungarian goulash, katsu curry shares space with Spanish grilled peppers. This book is a celebration of spiciness in every form: ingredients that turn the bland to the brilliant, the dreary into the divine.

And, like all food, it's the finest way to experience any foreign culture. Forget the funereal silence and air-conditioned gloom of those insipid 'international' restaurants, with their second-rate approximations of dreary Western fare. This is real food, pulsing with vibrancy and delight, bringing a truly happy tear to one's eye. You need nothing more than a healthy appetite, an open mind and a handful of the local currency. Spice. One word, a million different thrills.

DISHES

SPICINESS RATING   🌶 Mild 🌶🌶 Medium 🌶🌶🌶 Hot!

YOU'LL NEED

500g (1lb) ground lamb
500g (1lb) ground veal
1 red pepper, seeded and chopped
1 yellow onion, peeled and chopped
2 cloves of garlic, peeled and crushed
2 tsp red chilli flakes
2 tsp ground coriander
2 tsp ground cumin
2 tsp black pepper
3 tsp salt
2 red onions, peeled
1 tsp sumac
2 tsp lemon juice
1 cup (250mL) yoghurt
8 pieces of pita bread
4 tsp olive oil
Handful of parsley leaves

ORIGINS

Spicy lamb kebabs packed full of heat and flavour –and the essential unctuous tail fat – have long been popular across southeastern Anatolia, Syria and Iraq. But only in the Turkish city of Adana has the dish blending Turkish and Arab culinary influences been patented. Locals are so serious about it that sidewalk traders and more formal restaurants selling the dish are even subject to random inspections by the Adana Chamber of Commerce.

TURKEY

ADANA KEBAB

Smoky, spicy and supremely satisfying, it's worth a special trip to the somewhat off-the-beaten-track city of Adana just to taste Turkey's fieriest lamb kebab on its home turf.

METHOD

1 Mix the lamb and veal together in a large bowl, then stir in the red pepper, yellow onion and one clove of garlic.

2 Stir in the chilli flakes, coriander, cumin, pepper and two teaspoons of the salt, then cover and leave in the refrigerator, ideally overnight, but at least for a few hours.

3 Slice the red onions thinly, mix in the sumac and half the lemon juice; refrigerate overnight.

4 Mix the yoghurt with the remaining lemon juice, garlic and a teaspoon of salt, to create a sauce.

5 When it's time to cook, shape the meat mixture into cylinders around kebab skewers.

Your cylinders should measure about 15cm x 6cm (6in x 2in).

6 Place on a hot grill and cook for 3–4 minutes on each side. When the kebabs are ready, they should be slightly spongy to the touch.

7 Baste the pita bread with olive oil and place on the grill to warm through.

8 Place the kebab in the warm pita bread, add the sliced onions with sumac to the parsley, and garnish with the yoghurt sauce. If you like, serve with chargrilled tomatoes and red peppers.

TASTING NOTES

All your senses are aroused as you wend through the busy labyrinth of Adana's old town to dine on the city's signature dish. The call to prayer drifts from mosques and fragrant aromas waft from simple eateries concealed deep within the city's bazaar. Take a window seat with views of the compelling chaos outside and request *bir porsiyon* (one portion). Adana kebab is not a dish to be rushed and don't go making plans for dinner. Tear off some gossamer-thin bread, place some of the smoky, chargrilled lamb inside, and then stuff full of the zesty salad of parsley, onion and sumac. Repeat leisurely until you're satisfied; request a side order of grilled red peppers for an additional fiery hit. ● *by Brett Atkinson*

ORIGINS

Legend suggests this soy sauce-based fricassee was created in the 1980s in response to the surging popularity of fried chicken. The traditional way of serving chicken in market restaurants, boiled in a bland broth, was losing appeal. Creative minds in Andong had a Eureka moment: add some potatoes. Other suggestions followed and the idea for a new regional fare hatched: seasoned chicken casserole with veggies, glass noodles and a dollop of chilli peppers.

YOU'LL NEED

1.5kg (3lbs) chicken meat (thighs, wings and legs work well)
100g (3½oz) glass noodles (vermicelli)
¼ cup soy sauce
¼ cup oyster sauce (use more soy sauce if not available)
4 tbs rice syrup (corn syrup or honey)
1 tbs dark brown sugar
1–2 tbs minced garlic
1–2 tsp ginger, finely chopped
¼ tsp ground black pepper
2 cups water
4 medium potatoes, peeled and cut into chunks
1 medium carrot, sliced lengthways
1 medium onion, chopped
1 whole dried red chilli pepper, sliced
1–2 whole green chilli peppers, sliced
5–7 green onions, chopped
2 tsp sesame oil
1 tsp sesame seeds, to garnish

SERVES 4

SOUTH KOREA

ANDONG JJIMDAK

Chicken braised in a fiery sweet sauce: it's definitely not granny's Sunday casserole, but Andong *jjimdak* just might become your family's favourite weekend comfort food.

METHOD

1 Cook the chicken in boiling water for 1 minute to remove excess fat, then drain and set aside.

2 Soak the noodles in a bowl of warm water for 20 minutes, then drain.

3 Combine the soy sauce, oyster sauce, rice syrup, sugar, garlic, ginger and pepper in a bowl.

4 Place the chicken, sauce mixture and water in a wide pot and bring to the boil, then turn down to a medium heat, cover and cook for 10 minutes.

5 Add the potatoes, carrot and onion and simmer 10 minutes, keeping the lid on.

6 Add the drained noodles and chilli peppers and simmer for 7-10 minutes over a medium-high heat, until the sauce reduces by a third.

7 Remove from the heat and pour into a wide serving dish.

8 Stir in the sesame oil and sprinkle with sesame seeds. Serve.

TASTING NOTES

On a warm Saturday afternoon, the staff in the *jjimdak* restaurant near Busan's baseball stadium aren't in a hurry. There's a ball game on TV and the place will soon enough be packed with raucous fans looking for post-game drinks and a hearty meal. Graciously, the server takes the order and, thankfully, the owner points out the menu's hot pepper options. Minutes later, a wide serving dish arrives. It's brimming with chicken pieces, potatoes and carrots swimming in a garlicky sauce. Sure, it's a simple casserole, but the mélange of earthy flavours and the whiff of chilli pepper heat come together in a presentation that tickles the senses and inspires dinner guests to eagerly dig in. ● *by Rob Whyte*

ORIGINS

The dish's more famous cousin, chilli crab, emerged in the 1950s when Madam Cher's husband asked her to cook crabs differently. Instead of steaming, she stir-fried them in tomato sauce and chilli. The result was so good that she started serving seafood by the beach, before setting up Palm Beach seafood restaurant. A rival restaurant, Long Beach, started the black-pepper version in 1959. Today they are both possibly Singapore's most famed dishes.

SERVES 4

SINGAPORE

BLACK-PEPPER CRAB

**Everyone knows about Singapore's chilli crab but the other –
arguably tastier – crab dish worth seeking in the Lion City
is the version cooked in a spicy, black-pepper sauce.**

YOU'LL NEED

5 tbs coarsely ground black peppercorns
2 large crabs, quartered (Dungeness, Sri Lankan or mud varieties)
6 tbs unsalted butter
6 cloves of garlic, peeled and chopped
½ tsp ground white pepper
Pinch of Chinese five-spice powder
1 tbs oyster sauce
3 tbs Chinese rice wine
3 tbs water
Peanut oil

METHOD

1 In a wok, dry-fry the ground peppercorns on low heat to bring out the fragrance. Set aside.

2 Heat oil in a large wok over high heat until it starts shimmering.

3 Add the crab, ensuring that the heat remains high. Cook for 4–5 minutes and set aside. Drain the oil from the wok.

4 Reduce the heat to medium. Add the butter and fry the garlic, being careful not to burn them both.

5 Quickly add the black peppercorns, white pepper, five spice powder, oyster sauce, rice wine and water and mix.

6 Return the crab to the wok and stir to completely coat the crab in sauce. Remove and serve.

TASTING NOTES

While there's a certain romance in having seafood on a beach, good food can always trump the setting it's served in. And good food is just what this dish is: fresh crab, inherently sweet, tender and juicy, coated with a sticky, buttery pepper sauce – a hot wok is the key to combining the two elements. Of course, eating black-pepper crab is a messy affair: it's all fingers on deck when you crack the shell to slurp out the succulent flesh. While doing that, the peppery sauce tantalises your lips and tongue. Leave your white shirt at home and don't forget to wear a bib – it *will* get messy! ● *by Shawn Low*

YOU'LL NEED

15L (4 gallons) water
3–6 packages crab or
  crawfish boil
½ cup salt
½ cup hot sauce
6 tbsp cayenne pepper
450g (1½lbs) small red
  potatoes
10 small onions, peeled
8 ears corn, halved
12 asparagus spears
2 heads garlic, halved
1lb andouille sausage,
  chopped into 2.5cm (1in)
  chunks
6 large lemons, halved
4.5kg (10lbs) live crawfish

ORIGINS

The apocryphal story sees
lobsters slimming down when
following the French Canadians,
ancestors of modern Cajuns,
after they fled to Louisiana. The
reality? Native Americans likely
introduced crawfish to white
settlers. Well into the 1900s,
crawfish were fish bait and food
for the poor, but come 1960
with the Breaux Bridge Crawfish
Festival, and with the embrace
of Cajun culture in the 1970s and
1980s, crawfish became a well-
loved icon of Gulf Coast cuisine.

SERVES 5-6

GULF COAST, USA

BOILED CRAWFISH

'Mudbug' may not immediately stir your appetite, but don't be put off by this nickname for crawfish. When they're boiled right, these little crustaceans are like crimson fireworks of flavour.

METHOD

1 Fill a large pot with the water and add the spices, salt, hot sauce and cayenne pepper.

2 Cover and bring to a boil.

3 Place crawfish in a large container and fill with cool water. Stir to remove dirt from the crawfish, then transfer to a colander in small batches, and rinse under running water. Remove any dead crawfish or debris.

4 Once the water comes to a boil, add the potatoes, onions, corn, asparagus, garlic and sausage. Cover and cook for 10 minutes, or until the vegetables are tender.

5 Squeeze the lemons over the boil.

6 Add the crawfish, cover and cook for 3–5 minutes, until the shells are bright red. Remove from the heat and leave in the water for about 10 minutes.

7 Serve on newspaper.

TASTING NOTES

A 'boil' (or in local dialect, a 'berl') is both a method of cooking crawfish and the name for a social gathering that features boiled crawfish. Friends and family gather around enormous pots; sacks of crawfish are lowered into boiling water that is laced with corn, potatoes and whatever else is about, plus a load of spices. To be fair, the final product is not always hot – but it's certainly no surprise when a crawfish sears the tongue, and no boil is complete without plenty of beer, which both adds to the atmosphere and keeps mouths cooled off. Music is another inevitable accompaniment, and to this end, a good boil is the distillation of an outdoor Southern culinary gathering. ● *by Adam Karlin*

ORIGINS

Buffalo wings are said to be the invention of Teresa Bellissimo, part-owner of her family's Italian-American restaurant, Anchor Bar, in Buffalo, New York, which exists to this day. Family legend has it that Teresa whipped up the recipe from an oversupply of chicken wings as a late-night snack for her son's friends 50 years ago. The sauce has since evolved into a number of blends with different degrees of fieriness, but the original recipe remains a family secret.

**SERVES 4
(5 PIECES PER
PERSON)**

USA

BUFFALO WINGS

No bar menu, Super Bowl party or backyard barbecue is
complete without these fiery chicken snacks in hot-butter
sauce served with a blue-cheese dip and crunchy celery sticks.

YOU'LL NEED

10 chicken wings, wing tips
   removed, jointed to give 20
   pieces in total
½ cup (125mL) hot sauce
50g butter, melted
1 tbs Worcestershire sauce
1 tbs Tabasco sauce
1 tsp cayenne pepper
1 cup (250mL) sour cream
½ cup (125mL) mayonnaise
150g (5oz) blue cheese,
   crumbled
1 tbs white vinegar
Juice of 1 lemon
Seasoning to taste
Celery sticks to serve

METHOD

1 Marinate the chicken wings in a mixture of the hot sauce,
butter, Worcestershire sauce, Tabasco sauce and cayenne
pepper, preferably overnight.

2 Deep-fry or grill the wings until cooked and golden brown on
both sides.

3 Make the blue-cheese dip by combining the sour cream,
mayonnaise, blue cheese, white vinegar and lemon juice.
Season to taste.

4 Lay out the wings on a platter and serve with the dip and the
celery sticks.

TIP *This grilled version is less fiddly than the deep-fried
original but no less tasty. Anchor Bar publishes the recipe for
the original blue-cheese dip on its website, so check it out.*

TASTING NOTES

Like spaghetti and tacos, Buffalo wings are a no-no for important dining occasions, such as a
first date. There is simply no way to savour them other than using your fingers to coat hot and
sticky chicken with the unctuous blue-cheese dip. Cooling celery sticks provide the perfect
foil to the fiery sauce. Typically served on platters, the addictive combination of hot chilli
and soothing blue cheese means it is virtually impossible to stop at one. Serious Buffalo-wing
aficionados enter eating and cooking competitions across the country and debate the merits
or otherwise of deep-frying versus grilling; how hot the butter sauce should be; and whether
to use bottled blue-cheese dressing or a home-made version. ● *by Johanna Ashby*

ORIGINS

Myth surrounds the origin of Bunny Chow. Its geographical roots are clear, influenced by Durban's sizeable Indian population. But why did someone decide to scoop curry into a loaf of bread? Was it devised by Indian golf caddies in need of lunch in pre-Tupperware times? Or was it a restaurateur catering to people barred from certain eateries during apartheid? Whatever the answer, it is undeniably born of ingenuity.

YOU'LL NEED

Sunflower oil
2 onions, peeled and coarsely chopped
4 cardamom pods
1 stick cinnamon
4 curry leaves
2 tsp turmeric
4 tsp garam masala
2 tsp leaf masala
1 tsp ground coriander
2 tsp ground cumin
2 tsp grated fresh ginger
4 cloves of garlic, peeled and grated
800g (1lb 10oz) stewing lamb, preferably boneless, cut into bite-sized pieces
2 large tomatoes, coarsely chopped
2 potatoes, peeled and cubed
½ cup (125mL) water
1 tsp salt
Loaf of fresh white bread, unsliced
1 tin garden peas
Fresh coriander (cilantro) leaves to garnish

DURBAN, SOUTH AFRICA

BUNNY CHOW

Durban's home-grown dish has its roots in the subcontinent, but this fragrant, flavoursome curry comes served not with rice, roti or naan, but ladled into a hollowed-out loaf of bread.

METHOD

1 Add a generous glug of oil to a deep pan and fry the onions for 4–5 minutes on a medium heat.

2 Add the cardamom pods, cinnamon stick and curry leaves and fry until the onion begins to brown.

3 Add the turmeric, garam masala, leaf masala, ground coriander and cumin, then the ginger and garlic. Stir to coat the onion.

4 Cook for another couple of minutes, stirring constantly, then add the meat. If the oil has been soaked up by the spices, you can add a little extra oil.

5 Once the meat is starting to brown, add the tomatoes, potatoes and about ¼ cup (60mL) of hot water to start with, making sure that the potatoes are just covered with liquid. Stir in the salt.

6 Simmer for 30–40 minutes, until the meat and potatoes are tender. Add more liquid as required.

7 Prepare the bread, taking care to leave the crust intact and keeping a narrow lining of fluffy bread.

8 Add the tinned peas to the curry and heat for 5 minutes.

9 To serve, ladle the curry into each bread container and serve with a sprinkle of fresh coriander and the 'virgin' on the side.

TASTING NOTES

At first glance Bunny Chow seems an odd dish and you can't help wondering how to attack it without cutlery. But this fusion of Indian flavours with European bread is a culinary symbol of South Africa's melange of cultures. Eating it like a local presents a way to quickly assimilate into Durban life. As you munch through your Bunny, subdue the heat with the traditional can of cream soda, or spice it up with *atchar* (spicy pickles) or *sambal* (a salsa-like condiment). As you finish, use your 'virgin', the fluffy chunk of bread originally scooped out of the loaf, to mop up spilt juices – as a first-time Bunny eater, expect a little spillage. ● *by Lucy Corne*

SERVES 6

ORIGINS

Chillies, native to the New World, have been cultivated in Latin America for some 6000 years, and tomatoes are also native. Garlic and onions, however, were brought to Mexico by the Spaniards in the 16th century, so the dish must have been created after this time. Though the precise origins of the *a la diabla* preparation are unknown, it is especially popular in the coastal regions of the Yucatan peninsula and the West Coast.

MEXICO

CAMARONES A LA DIABLA

This frisky dish of shrimp (*camarones*) cooked in a lava-like tomato sauce gets its name, '*a la diabla*' – devil-style! – from the punch packed by the many, many chillies it contains.

YOU'LL NEED

4 cups (1L) water
5 medium tomatoes, chopped
2 medium red onions, peeled and sliced
6 cloves of garlic, peeled
400g (14oz) canned chipotle chillies
2¾ cups (700mL) ketchup
1 tsp salt
2 tbs vegetable oil
1kg (2lb) peeled shrimp

METHOD

1 Put the water, tomatoes, half an onion and the garlic cloves in a large pot.

2 Bring to the boil over a high heat, then reduce to a simmer and cook until the tomatoes are soft.

3 Remove from heat and allow to cool for 2 minutes.

4 Pour the tomato mixture into a blender, adding the chillies, ketchup and salt. Blend until smooth.

5 Saute the remaining onion in a pan with the vegetable oil over medium-high heat until golden brown. Add the shrimp and cook for 2 minutes.

6 Pour the tomato sauce over the shrimp and simmer for 8 minutes.

7 Serve over rice.

TASTING NOTES

Imagine sitting at a beach cantina in, oh, say, the Yucatan town of Tulum or the Oaxacan coastal hamlet of Mazunte, your bare feet skimming the warm, white sand. You're a few margaritas in when the waiter brings you a plate of *camarones a la diabla* – fat pink shrimp swimming in a brilliant-red sauce, its surface gleaming with butter. You tear off a piece of hot corn tortilla and scoop up a bite. The fiery kick of the chilli contrasts with the firmness of the shrimp, making your mouth water. You cool everything down with a bite of rice or *frijoles refritos* (refried beans) flecked with white queso fresco (fresh cheese), then go in for more fire. Devillishly good. ● *by Emily Matchar*

ORIGINS

The ubiquity of curry in the Caribbean is thanks to a large population of Indo-Caribbeans, mostly descendants of indentured sugarcane workers brought to the region in colonial days. Common Indian curry spices – turmeric, coriander, cumin – were supplemented with native Caribbean allspice, which gives the dish a unique, warm flavour. The heat comes from the Scotch bonnet chilli, known in Guyana as the Ball of Fire – about three times hotter than tongue-scorching cayenne.

YOU'LL NEED

2 tsp curry powder
½ tsp allspice
2 onions, peeled and diced
2 spring onions (scallions), roughly chopped
½ tsp salt
½ tsp pepper
2 Scotch bonnet chillies (or 4 jalapeño chillies), thinly sliced
1 tbs grated fresh ginger
Water
1kg (2lb) goat stewing meat, cubed
1 tbs butter
2 medium potatoes, diced
2 medium carrots, sliced
Steamed rice to serve

SERVES 4

CARIBBEAN

CARIBBEAN CURRY GOAT

A party in Jamaica or Trinidad is not considered complete without a steaming pot of curry goat, a highly spiced stew of goat meat spiked with flaming-hot Scotch bonnet chillies.

METHOD

1 Combine curry powder, allspice, onions, spring onions, salt, pepper, chillies, ginger and cup (125mL) of water in a blender and blend for approximately 30 seconds.

2 Rub the mixture over the meat and refrigerate in a plastic bag or sealed container overnight.

3 Drain the meat, reserving the remaining marinade.

4 Melt the butter in a large pan over medium-high heat then brown the goat pieces.

5 Add the potatoes, carrots, marinade and enough water to cover the meat.

6 Bring to the boil, then simmer until tender (1–2 hours).

7 Serve with steamed rice.

TASTING NOTES

While curry goat is on the menu of many home-style Caribbean restaurants, it's best known as a party dish. Any large gathering – a birthday celebration, a village dance, a Christmas party – necessitates the presence of a curry goat 'specialist' to prepare and stir the stew as the festivities begin. Partygoers, tired from dancing and rum-guzzling, grab paper plates piled with rice and curry to revive them as steel drums pound in the background. The slow-stewed meat is pleasantly chewy, the sauce deep and complex. The heat comes on slowly, rolling from the back of your tongue to the front, building to a crescendo. Revellers muffle the heat with rice, or, in Trinidad, Indian-style roti bread. ● *by Emily Matchar*

ORIGINS

The roots of *ceviche* go back to Incan times when *chicha*, a marinated corn drink, was used to flavour fish prior to cooking. The lime was introduced to Latin America by Spanish conquistadores, proving a sublime match for the white fish of South America's Pacific coast. Some also believe that ocean-going navigators from Polynesian islands introduced a version of the dish to Easter Island and continental South America. Dishes such as Rarotonga's *ika mata* are very similar.

YOU'LL NEED

1 red onion, peeled and thinly sliced

1kg (2lb) fillets of firm white fish (eg sea bass) cut into large bite-sized chunks

1 pinch red chilli flakes

3 cloves of garlic, peeled and finely chopped

½ cup (125mL) fresh lime juice

3 tbs olive oil

2 tsp rice vinegar

¼ tsp caster sugar

1 Peruvian *aji limo* chilli, seeded and chopped (substitute a small red chilli if not available)

2 sweetcorn cobs cut in half

2 sweet potatoes, peeled and sliced thinly

3 tbs chopped fresh coriander (cilantro) leaves

Salt

Ground black pepper

PACIFIC COAST, PERU

CEVICHE

Combining a Spanish-influenced citrus and coriander (cilantro) punch with marinated raw fish and chillies used in Incan times, Peru's national dish has now been adopted and adapted across Latin America.

METHOD

1 Layer half of the sliced onions in a glass bowl and lay the fish on top. Sprinkle on the chilli flakes and chopped garlic and cover with lime juice.

2 Cover the bowl and place in a refrigerator to marinate for 2 hours. During this time spoon the lime juice over the fish two more times.

3 Whisk together 2 tbs of the oil, rice vinegar and caster sugar until smooth, then add the chopped fresh chilli.

4 After the fish has been marinated, drain and discard the lime juice and stir in the mixture of chilli/oil/rice vinegar/caster sugar, blending well.

5 Preheat a grill to medium.

6 Brush the sweetcorn and sweet potato with the remaining oil and place under the grill for 10–15 minutes, turning frequently until cooked and lightly charred.

7 Divide the *ceviche* into six servings. Top with chopped coriander and the remaining sliced red onion, and season to taste with salt and ground black pepper.

8 Serve with the grilled sweetcorn and sweet potato.

TASTING NOTES

On a continent where food can be heavy with carbs – rice, beans and potatoes anyone? – the lightness of flavour of *ceviche* is a revelation. Visually, it's also a diverse treat with red and green accents of chilli and coriander standing out on the neutral canvas of white fish punctuated by the pink of finely chopped red onion. Your first mouthful will boldly announce the super-fresh crunch of the onions and the sharp punch of lime juice. Then the chilli fire hits, but it's balanced with the freshness of the fish and a subtle sweetness from a touch of sugar, creating an exciting epicurean experience like no other. ● *by Brett Atkinson*

YOU'LL NEED

500g boneless chicken, cut
  into chunks
1 tsp ginger, grated
1 tsp garlic, crushed
10 curry leaves
5-6 whole green chillies
1 cup vegetable oil
1 tbs coriander, chopped

For the marinade

2 tsp of red Kashmiri chilli
  powder
1 tsp grated ginger
1 tsp crushed garlic
½ tsp turmeric powder
½ tsp ground black pepper
1 tbs lemon juice
Pinch of salt

For the sauce

1 cup natural yoghurt
1 tsp of red Kashmiri chilli
  powder
½ tsp of red food colouring
½ tsp turmeric powder
½ tsp coriander powder
Pinch of salt

For the batter

1 egg
2 tbs of cornflour
1 tbs of rice flour
1 tbs water

ORIGINS

When A. M. Buhari, the
proprietor of Chennai's Buhari
Hotel, invented Chicken 65 in
1965, he had no idea what he
was starting. The civic-minded
hotelier decided not to patent
the recipe for his phenomenally
popular chicken snack and
hawkers took it to the streets in
droves. Buhari didn't stop there
– Chicken 65 was followed by
Chicken 78 in 1978, Chicken 82
in 1982 and Chicken 90 in 1990.

SERVES 4

CHICKEN 65

Chennai's favourite non-veg snack is devil red, and devilishly spicy – the perfect accompaniment to a cold Kingfisher on a steamy South Indian afternoon.

METHOD

1 Mix all the marinade ingredients together in a stain-proof bowl and combine with the chicken until thoroughly coated. Allow to marinate for at least an hour.

2 Combine all the sauce ingredients in a bowl, and set aside.

3 For the batter, beat the egg and combine with the other batter ingredients until they form a smooth paste; stir together with the marinated chicken.

4 In a wok, heat a cup of vegetable oil and deep-fry the chicken on a medium flame till golden. Set aside on a piece of kitchen towel to absorb the excess oil.

5 Discard the frying oil and add 2 tbs of fresh vegetable oil to your pan. Saute the ginger and garlic for a few seconds until aromatic then add the curry leaves and green chillies and the battered chicken pieces.

6 Add the yoghurt mixture and cook on a medium flame until it is almost absorbed and the chicken pieces are almost dry.

7 Garnish your devil-red chicken pieces with chopped coriander and serve.

TASTING NOTES

You can still find the original Chicken 65 at the restaurant where it was invented, but the street-side offering is just as delicious. And even in its streetwise incarnation, this is one snack that looks great on a plate – candy apple-red chicken pieces tossed together with whole green chillies, curry leaves and chopped coriander. Perfect Chicken 65 should be served straight from the pan, still sizzling but moist and tender inside its chilli and spice jacket. The flavours should hit you in waves – chilli, garlic, ginger, pepper, coriander. It's lip-smackingly good and will leave a tingle on your lips that is best quenched with an ice-cold bottle of Kingfisher. ● *by Joe Bindloss*

ORIGINS

Frankfurters hail from Frankfurt, but the resemblance between these and the American hot dog, may only be skin deep. Chilli has existed since prehistoric man (or woman) discovered that mixing spicy chilli peppers into past-its-best meat made it taste better. Where the marriage between sausage and spicy-as-hell beef chili first occurred is debated: California, Michigan and Brooklyn's Coney Island all claim the honour. Whatever, the result is darn delicious.

YOU'LL NEED

6 cloves of garlic, peeled and chopped
1 large yellow onion, peeled and chopped
Olive oil
500g (1lb) ground beef
2 tbs cayenne pepper
2 tbs chilli powder
2 tbs smoked paprika
1 tbs cumin
1 tsp salt
225g (8oz) can of tomato sauce
2 tbs honey
20 hot dogs and buns
1 large red onion (to garnish), peeled and finely chopped
110g (¼lb) shredded extra-mature (extra-sharp) cheese

MAKES 20 CHILLI DOGS

USA

CHILLI DOGS

Take an old-world food (the hot dog), slap it in a bun, ladle on smokin'-hot chili made with spices indigenous to the American Southwest, and – *voilà!* – quintessential Americana.

METHOD

1 Sauté the chopped garlic and yellow onion in a little olive oil over a medium heat for about 10–15 minutes, until soft and translucent.

2 Stir in the ground beef along with the cayenne pepper, chilli powder, smoked paprika and cumin and stir-fry for about 10 minutes, until the meat is browned.

3 Add the salt, tomato sauce and honey, reduce the heat to low and simmer, covered, for an hour, stirring occasionally.

4 Once the chilli is ready, grill or boil the hot dogs and grill or toast the buns.

5 Place a hot dog in each of the buns, ladle over some chilli and garnish with chopped red onion and cheese.

TASTING NOTES

Traditional Tex-Mex chilli is an explosion of meat and spice that works brilliantly slathered on top of a beef dog, tempered slightly by extra-sharp cheese and topped with the additional crispy tang of raw red onion. Though easy to find (in America, at least) making your own chilli dogs allows you to indulge in variation. Not a fan of processed meats? Use sausages prepared by a local butcher. Red meat not your thing? The entire dish can be made with turkey. Vegetarians can even use soy-dogs and chilli made with texturized vegetable protein (TVP). Some folks split the dog down the middle, but keeping them intact gives a more satisfying juicy meat-bomb mouth-feel. ● *by Joshua Samuel Brown*

ORIGINS

The chorizo is a post-Columbian snag, appearing sometime in the 1600s. This is because the main flavouring, paprika, is a New World spice. Still, it's changed little since its inception: paprika-spiced pork and fat stuffed into a large or small intestine. It's now devoured all over Spain and Portugal, as well as the various Central and South American countries that were conquered by these empires.

TASTING NOTES

Ah, the charred snap of a perfectly grilled chorizo. The meat should be charred and glistening with scarlet juice, the flesh suitably piggy and the paprika strong, but never overwhelming. Some like theirs *picante* (or hot), while others prefer *dolce* (sweet), where the flavours are a little more muted. If you can find outlets that specialise in their own recipe, so much the better; the difference between a cheap, mass-produced version and a handmade beauty is huge. The cooked version is thinly sliced and crammed into *boccadillos* (small sandwiches). It, too, can vary in taste and pungency. But for the true experience of chorizo, they're best eaten burning hot, straight from the grill. ● *by Tom Parker Bowles*

SPAIN/PORTUGAL

CHORIZO

Gloriously fatty cured pork, garlic and paprika sausage, available cooked, raw, sweet or hot. Slice into sandwiches, fry with eggs, or simply grill... it's one of the world's great bangers.

FABADA

This is a rich, Spanish bean stew featuring chorizo, traditionally from the Asturia region. Enjoy with traditional accompaniments of crusty bread and apple cider.

YOU'LL NEED

1 cup dry haricot (navy) beans, soaked overnight
6 cloves of garlic, peeled
2 medium onions, peeled and quartered
1 bay leaf
4 tbs extra virgin olive oil
450g (1lb) streaky bacon
160g (6oz) black pudding
3 chorizo sausages
1 small rump roast or several small pork ribs
Pinch of saffron threads
1 tbs sweet paprika
Salt (optional)

METHOD

1 Drain the beans and place them in a large pot of cold water (cover the beans by about 5cm/2in) with the garlic, onions and bay leaf and bring to the boil.

2 Add the olive oil, bacon, black pudding, chorizo, rump roast/pork ribs. Half-cover the pot with a lid and simmer for 1½ hours.

3 Add the saffron threads and paprika and simmer for another 1–1½ hours.

4 Taste and add salt if necessary, but it may be okay without more, given the saltiness of the sausage and bacon.

5 Remove the sausage, black pudding and roast from the pot, cut them into serving-size pieces then return them to the pot.

6 Ladle into soup bowls and eat steaming hot.

YOU'LL NEED

300g (11oz) bulgur
1¼ cups (300mL) water
1 large onion, peeled and
  chopped
300g (11oz) beef (or lamb),
  finely ground and as lean as
  possible
2 tbs tomato paste
Bunch of parsley, chopped
1 tbs cinnamon
1 tbs cumin
Juice of 1 lemon
100g (3oz) *isot* pepper, or
  ground chilli flakes
1 lettuce to serve (cos lettuce
  works well)
Lemon segments, to serve

ORIGINS

Çiğ köfte is said to originate
from Urfa, on the edge of the
Mesopotamian plain, during
Biblical times when King Nimrod
piled all of the area's firewood
into an execution pyre for his
nemesis, the prophet Abraham.
Left with no fuel for cooking,
a local woman ground together
a mixture of raw meat, bulgur and
spices. According to the story,
Abraham walked from the flames
unharmed, and the dish gained
lasting fame from its walk-on
role in the legendary tale.

SERVES 4

TURKEY

ÇİĞ KÖFTE

Çiğ köfte is a gritty, raw-meat and cracked-wheat experience, buzzing with the scorching *isot* pepper of the Mesopotamian plains that 'cooks' the raw ingredients, all served in a lettuce leaf.

METHOD

1 Place the bulgur, water and chopped onion in a large bowl. Mix together with your hands for up to 15 minutes until the bulgur softens.

2 Add the ground meat, tomato paste and chopped parsley, mixing to ensure all ingredients are evenly dispersed.

3 While continuing to roll and knead for up to 30 minutes, progressively add cinnamon, cumin, lemon juice and *isot* (or ground chilli flakes). Experienced *çiğ köfte*-makers will turn and fold their mixture constantly, periodically adding more *isot*, chopped parsley or lemon juice, and working to get as smooth a consistency as possible.

4 Serve by placing a dollop of the mixture on lettuce leaves and dressing with a squeeze of lemon (and more *isot* if you are bold).

TASTING NOTES

Generally served as a make-your-own communal appetiser, *çiğ köfte* requires its own eating technique. Taking a lettuce leaf, spread it with the spicy-meaty mixture, drizzle with lemon juice, then – if you dare – add more *isot* pepper, and eat. The crisp lettuce is your first encounter, before you experience the creamy, meaty essence of the ground beef that is the core of the dish, also noticing the slight grittiness of the bulgur. Soon the peppery fire of *isot* will dawn on you, a slow smouldering that builds to a furnace-like intensity. This is your cue to reach for more cooling lettuce, or extra drizzles of lemon. Or to embrace the fire and wolf down more. ● *by Will Gourlay*

ORIGINS

Pepper has been cultivated in Cambodia for over a thousand years. From French colonial times Kampot's pepper was regarded as the world's finest by Parisian chefs. The Vietnam War and the Khmer Rouge era halted production, but Kampot pepper is reassuming its global renown. Most is exported in dried form, but the just-picked unripe berry has a zingy, citrusy flavour that's perfect with stir-fried crab.

YOU'LL NEED

2 tbs peanut oil
4–6 whole crabs (ideally mud or blue swimmer crabs)
3 cloves of garlic, peeled and coarsely chopped
3 tsp finely chopped fresh ginger
4 Kampot green peppercorn vines (available in Asian grocery stores or online), or 2 tbs green peppercorns in brine, drained and carefully rinsed
1½ tsp fish sauce
2 tbs soy sauce
2 tsp palm sugar
6 spring onions (scallions), trimmed on the ends and sliced diagonally into chunks
Steamed rice to serve

SERVES 2-4

CRAB WITH KAMPOT PEPPER

Stir-fried crab with Kampot pepper, ginger and garlic is one of Southeast Asia's tastiest dishes, best enjoyed while listening to the sea, close to the source of its super-fresh ingredients.

METHOD

1 Heat the oil over high heat in a hot wok until it's almost smoking. Add the whole crabs and stir-fry for around 5 minutes until almost cooked.

2 Add the garlic, ginger and peppercorns, and stir-fry for a minute until soft and fragrant.

3 Add the fish sauce, soy sauce and palm sugar and stir-fry for 2-3 minutes until the sauce thickens.

4 Remove from the heat and stir in the sliced spring onions until they wilt.

5 Serve over steamed rice.

TASTING NOTES

When Cambodia was a French colony, Kep was a beach escape for the French residents of Phnom Penh. With a compact waterfront corniche, it still retains a Gallic ambience but the town's famous crab market could only be in Southeast Asia. Fresh crabs are landed by fishermen in the morning and then it's just a short distance to hot woks. Eating crab initially looks challenging, but using a tiny fork makes it easy to extract the tender meat inside the shell and legs. The overriding flavour is the fragrant zing of green peppercorns, with a subtle saltiness and sweet notes coming from fish sauce and palm sugar. Ocean breezes and chilled Angkor beer complete one of Cambodia's best dining experiences. ● *by Brett Atkinson*

ORIGINS

Peru's fusion history can be traced through *cau cau*. For centuries, the humble potato was unknown to the world except in Peru in 3800 varieties. Then the Spanish conquistadors stomped in and feasted on beef, leaving their African and indigenous slaves what was left in the kitchen – tripe, potatoes, spearmint and spicy *ají*. It's likely the Chinese and Italians added their own twists centuries later, with the additions of turmeric and rice on the side.

SERVES 4

COASTAL PERU

CREOLE CAU CAU

Peru's African, Chinese and Andean histories sing a story to your tastebuds in this creole stew. Yellow *ají* chillies high five turmeric for a golden sauce over potatoes and seafood or chicken (or the more traditional tripe).

YOU'LL NEED

⅓ cup vegetable oil
½ cup red onion, chopped
2 garlic cloves, chopped
2 yellow *ají* (or other chilli as a
  last resort)
1 tsp turmeric
½ tsp cumin
salt and pepper, to taste
1kg seafood (squid, mussels,
  prawns; or tripe or chicken),
  diced
4 cups fish stock
4 medium potatoes, peeled
  and diced
1 cup peas
4 tbs spearmint (or mint),
  chopped
rice, to serve

METHOD

1 Sauté the onion and garlic in the oil until brown.

2 Add the *ají*, turmeric, cumin and seasoning, and cook for 5 minutes.

3 Add the seafood, stock, potatoes, peas and 3 tablespoons of the spearmint. If using tripe, precook it with milk and water.

4 Simmer until the potatoes are tender.

5 Garnish with spearmint and serve with rice.

TASTING NOTES

You're in a Ma and Pa restaurant in Miraflores, Lima, and the first bite of *cau cau* has the comfort of an Indian curry, but with a simplicity all its own. The radio plays tinny music. The smell of ocean salt is in the air, as always; imagine the journey across the waters that brought this union of flavours to Peru's capital. The *ají amarillo* ('yellow' chilli) is a tiny powerhouse, punching with spice above its four inches. Its pungent flavour adds depth, so it's not overbearingly spicy, but plays nicely with the turmeric and cumin. The rice tempers everything. It's a spicy ride, all washed down with *chicha morada*, a purple maize drink drunk for millennia before the Spanish landed. ● *by Phillip Tang*

ORIGINS

In Chinese days of yore, street vendors carried their kitchens in baskets hanging on *dan dan* – bamboo poles slung across their shoulders. At the request of hungry passers-by, this could be unharnessed and used to prepare a fast-food noodle feast. The unique spicy-nutty noodle concoction soon became known as *dan dan* noodles, which translates as 'peddler's noodles'.

YOU'LL NEED

300g (11oz) fresh egg noodles
2 cloves of garlic, peeled
5cm (2in) piece of fresh
  ginger, peeled
3 spring onions (scallions),
  white and green parts
2 tbs peanut oil
200g (7oz) minced fatty pork
  (or beef)
1 tbs Shaoxing Chinese rice
  wine
Salt
Handful of dry-roasted
  peanuts, roughly chopped

Sauce

3 tsp water
2 tbs light soy sauce
3 tbs tahini or sesame paste
1 tbs Chinese black rice
  vinegar
2–3 tbs chilli oil (adjust for
  chilli hit)
2 tsp sesame oil
1 tsp sugar
1 tsp ground Sichuan pepper

TASTING NOTES

Sichuan restaurants are sweat-inducing places packed with punters and bubbling bowls of chilli concoctions. Take a deep breath. Locals like to see a foreigner reeling after a mouthful of their native food, in which case *dan dan* noodles is a good option. Its mid-range spiciness is right on the money, with the different textures of noodles, meat and stauce contributing to varying levels of heat. The punch to watch for is the Sichuan pepper. It creeps up on the palate like a tourist to a panda, creating a tingling or anaesthetised *ma-la* sensation, which is as addictive as the chilli hit. Seeing red? Water won't help – the only answer is to keep slurping. ● *by Penny Watson*

CHINA

DAN DAN NOODLES

This Sichuan dish comprises yellow egg noodles tossed in a red chilli, Sichuan pepper and sesame sauce, topped with minced pork (or beef) fried with aromatics, and finished with peanuts.

METHOD

1 Bring a large pot of lightly salted water to the boil.

2 Cook the noodles for 3–5 minutes until al dente.

3 Rinse under cold water, then drain and tip into a serving dish.

4 In a small bowl, whisk together all the sauce ingredients.

5 Pour the sauce over the noodles and toss. Set aside.

6 In a mortar, pound the garlic, ginger and two of the spring onions.

7 Heat the oil in a frying pan over medium-high heat. Add the garlic, ginger and spring onion paste and fry briefly until fragrant. Add

the meat and stir-fry until it is no longer pink and the pan gets sticky.

8 Deglaze with rice wine and season with salt.

9 Spoon the cooked meat mixture over the noodles, sprinkle with remaining chopped spring onion and the peanuts. Serve straight away.

ORIGINS

The history of *wat* and *injera* remain a mystery, although we do know that the ox and plough have been used in Ethiopia for at least 3000 years and that *teff*, the essential behind *injera*, is probably as old. *Wat* – the name for an array of curries – has been consumed in some form for just as long, although the dish didn't gain its legendary bite until the Portuguese introduced the chilli in the 16th century.

YOU'LL NEED

Berbere Spice mixture

1 tsp ground ginger
½ tsp cardamom seeds
½ tsp fenugreek seeds
½ tsp ground coriander seeds
½ tsp ground cinnamon
¼ tsp ground cloves
¼ tsp allspice
2 tbs salt
½ cup cayenne pepper
½ cup sweet paprika

Doro Wat

4 tbs *nit'r qibe* (Ethiopian spiced butter) or unsalted butter
2 large onions, peeled and roughly chopped
1 tbs peeled and chopped garlic
1 tbs peeled and finely chopped
1–2 tbs *berbere* (to taste)
4 chicken legs
Salt
4 hard-boiled eggs
Injera

TASTING NOTES

There is an art to eating *doro wat*. First, do away with plates, bowls and utensils and instead pile the *wat* on to a sheet of *injera*. On to what, you might ask? Unique to Ethiopia, *injera* can best be described as a large, thin, rubbery and rather sour-tasting fermented pancake made of *teff*, a cereal that grows only in the Ethiopian highlands. The *injera* serves as accompaniment, cutlery and, some would say, tablecloth to your *wat*; its bitter tang tempers the fire of the *wat*. In order to make your Ethiopian meal even more authentic, finish off with a brain-bendingly strong Ethiopian coffee (Ethiopia is the original home of the coffee plant). ● *by Stuart Butler*

ETHIOPIA

DORO WAT

**Wrap some tangy *injera* (fermented pancake) around
a morsel of *doro wat*, a devilishly hot chicken stew, pop it
into your mouth and savour the tastes of highland Ethiopia.**

METHOD

Berbere Spice mixture

1 Heat a large, heavy pan.

2 Add the ginger, cardamom, fenugreek, coriander, cinnamon, cloves and allspice; roast over a low heat for 2 minutes, stirring constantly to prevent burning.

3 Add the salt, cayenne pepper and paprika and roast over very low heat for a further 10 minutes.

4 Allow to cool; store in a sealed jar.

Doro Wat

1 Heat the butter over a low heat in a large wok or deep frying pan.

2 Add the onions and, stirring frequently for about 25 minutes, cook until caramelised.

3 Add the garlic and ginger and cook for 5–8 minutes, until soft.

4 Add the *berbere* and 2 cups (500mL) of water. Stir well.

5 Season the chicken with salt.

6 Add the chicken to the wok, cover and simmer for about 40 minutes, stirring

occasionally, until cooked through.

7 Uncover the wok and raise the heat to medium-high.

8 Simmer until the liquid has been reduced to a thick, gravy-like consistency.

9 Add the eggs and stir to warm them through.

10 Taste and season with more *berbere* and salt.

11 Serve with *injera* and eat with the fingers.

ORIGINS

Chilli peppers hark from the Americas, of course, but spread rapidly through Asia from the 16th century, probably arriving in Bhutan a couple of centuries later. But whereas in India chillies are used mainly to add heat to dishes, in this long-isolated Himalayan kingdom *ema* are considered vegetables – the core component of *ema datse* and an integral part of almost every other dish, though also served as condiments.

SERVES 4

BHUTAN

EMA DATSE

Not so much a national dish as a national obsession: in Bhutan, *ema datse* is ubiquitous – a palpitation-inducing chillies-and-cheese combo that's much more than the sum of its parts.

YOU'LL NEED

250g (9oz) large chillies, sliced
   lengthwise into four
200g (7oz) soft cheese
1 medium onion or a handful
   of spring onions (scallions),
   diced
½ cup (125mL) water
4 tbs oil
Salt to taste
Rice to serve

METHOD

1 Place all of the ingredients in a medium saucepan and cook on a low heat for 10–15 minutes till the cheese has formed a smooth sauce with the water and oil.

2 Serve with rice. That's it.

3 For reduced tongue-burn, remove the seeds and membranes from the chillies before cooking, and consider adding chopped tomato or other vegetables. Alternatively, if you'd prefer it turned up to 11, heat the water before adding the other ingredients.

TIP *Choose chillies to suit your taste: large green ones give crunch and freshness, reds heat, dried chillies intensity. In Bhutan, home-made cow's-milk cheese is used, or rounds of cottage cheese bought at markets and roadside stalls; you can use pretty much any soft or medium-hard variety.*

TASTING NOTES

Whether you're in a swanky hotel restaurant or a traditional farmhouse kitchen, *ema datse* is not just customary, it's mandatory. Peer through the gloom (Bhutanese curtains are always closed) and pile the favoured red rice on your plate. Add a ladleful of dried beef stewed with – of course – chillies; in spring, you might also be treated to fresh asparagus or nakey (fern fronds). Finally, top with a dollop of *ema datse*, and dive in. First, enjoy the crunch of sliced chillies, sweet and earthy; savour the contrast with the thick, rich cheese sauce as it folds around your tongue. Then reach for the Red Panda wheat beer and prepare to douse the oral conflagration. Repeat till sated and sweaty. ● *by Sarah Baxter*

ORIGINS

Dipping lightly fried corn tortillas in salsa, or pouring salsa over them, may have been a culinary accident in pre-Hispanic Mexico (that is, before the arrival of Spanish conquistadores), or perhaps a genius move by hungry tribesmen. In any case, the domestic cultivation of maize or corn thousands of years ago allowed the creation of tortillas, and it is likely that somebody has been making some kind of *enchilada* ever since.

YOU'LL NEED

10 tomatillos, husked

3–4 serrano chillies or 2–3 jalapeños

2–3 sprigs of fresh coriander (cilantro)

1 small onion, peeled and cut in chunks

1 clove of garlic, peeled

2 tbs canola oil

2 cups (500mL) chicken or vegetable stock

Salt

2 tbs canola oil

4 corn tortillas

1 large chicken breast, cooked and shredded

¼ cup (60mL) thick cream or sour cream

½ cup (125mL) *queso añejo* or mild parmesan

1-2 onions, peeled and sliced into rings

SERVES 2

MEXICO & SOUTHWESTERN USA

ENCHILADAS

To *enchilar* means to put chilli on something, which is precisely what you do with this dish of tortillas stuffed with chicken, beef, pork or eggs and slathered in chilli salsa.

METHOD

1 Boil the tomatillos and chillies in salted water for 10 minutes. Drain.

2 Puree the soaked tomatillos and chillies, coriander, onion and garlic to make a salsa. This should make around 2½ cups (625mL) of tomatillo sauce.

3 Heat 1 tbs oil in a frying pan over a medium–high heat. Pour in the salsa and stir for 5 minutes; it will get darker and thicker.

4 Add the chicken or vegetable stock and salt to taste, reduce the heat and simmer for 10 minutes. Keep warm.

5 Heat the remaining oil in a small frying pan and fry the tortillas quickly. You want to soften the tortillas but don't let them get too crispy. Drain on paper towels.

6 Pour a couple of tablespoons of the salsa on to a plate. Lay a tortilla over it and put some of the shredded chicken in the centre. Roll up. Repeat with 3 more tortillas.

7 Cover the *enchiladas* with salsa.

8 Sprinkle the *enchiladas* with cheese, a dollop of cream and onion and serve.

TASTING NOTES

Enchiladas verdes (green *enchiladas*) are perhaps the most widely available *enchiladas* in Mexico. Often eaten for dinner at unpretentious restaurants, it's a seemingly simple dish that hides its complex blend of flavours and textures. Like most *enchiladas*, half the fun comes from the salsa and this one, made of tangy *tomatillos*, (a light-green berry), serrano or jalapeño chillies and a sprig of coriander (cilantro), has potency and a hint of sweetness. The tortillas are filled with poached shredded chicken and topped with sliced onions and sharp Mexican cheese (such as *queso añejo*) so that every bite offers six layers of greatness: tangy, spicy, a bit sweet, crunchy (from the onions and the tortillas), sharp (from the cheese) and juicy chicken. ● *by Mauricio Velázquez de León*

ORIGINS

Fiš paprikas harks back to the
Austro-Hungarian empire and
is influenced by the cuisine
of Croatia's northeastern
neighbour, Hungary. In the
Croatian region of Slavonia, fish
such as trout, carp and catfish
populate the Drava, Sava and
Danuba rivers that carve up the
land. The dish combines the
resources available in the region
– freshwater fish, homegrown
paprika, farm-fresh chilli
peppers and springwater – to
make a deceptively simple soup.

SERVES 2

CROATIA

FIŠ PAPRIKAS

Croatia's love for fresh fish meets Hungary's goulash traditions in this fiery fish broth from northeastern Croatia. This is a hot, hearty take on the traditional 'catch of the day'.

YOU'LL NEED

Olive oil
2 onions, peeled and diced
2 tbs tomato paste
Pinch of salt
2 tbs hot paprika
Large freshwater fish (trout, carp, catfish or pike), cleaned and cut into pieces
1 stock or bouillon cube
¼ cup (60mL) white wine
Handful of cut hot pepper
Packet of wide egg noodlest

METHOD

1 Put the onions in a pan with a splash of olive oil and saute over a medium heat for about 10 minutes.

2 Add the tomato paste, salt, paprika, fish, stock or bouillon cube and 6 cups (1.5L) of water per kilo of prepared fish.

3 Simmer over a medium heat for about 15 minutes.

4 Add the wine and cut hot pepper, and cook for another 30 minutes over a low heat. The sauce should have a rich, broth-like consistency.

5 Cook the noodles in hot boiling water.

6 Pour the sauce over the noodles and serve.

TASTING NOTES

At the annual *fiš paprikas* competition held every July in Slavonski Brod, hundreds of participants line the river Sava with iron-cast cauldrons and buckets of freshly netted fish. If you don't own a cauldron, you can make *fiš paprika* on a household burner or hob. Catfish is a favourite in the region; aficionados say its flakes are softer in the mouth than those of carp or trout. The taste is enhanced by cut hot pepper and paprika. Opt for a mixture of sweet and hot paprika if you can; for *fiš paprikas*, locals love the sweet, delicate *kulonleges* variety, mixed with the self-explanatory *eros* classification. The resulting dish is comforting and warming, with spice laced through the flakes of fish. ● *by Kate Thomas*

ORIGINS

As with many Peranakan dishes, the roots of fish head curry can be traced back to the early days of nautical migration and trade between East Asia, South Asia and the West. While today's dish might seem, at first glance, more heavily influenced by its South rather than East Asian roots, the Chinese fondness for fish head is well known, making the Peranakan version – like Singapore itself – a shining example of cultural cooperation.

YOU'LL NEED

2 tbs oil

1 tsp fenugreek seeds

3 sprigs curry leaves

3 cloves of garlic, finely chopped

2 onions, peeled and thinly sliced

6–8 small pickled red chillies, diced

3 tbs madras curry powder

2 tbs tamarind paste

Salt to taste

1 large (about 1kg/2lb) red snapper head

8 large okra, cut lengthwise

225g (½lb) fried tofu, cubed

2 big tomatoes cut into quarters

1 cup (250mL) coconut milk

1 tbs chopped fresh coriander (cilantro) leaves

2 cups (500mL) water

SERVES 4

SINGAPORE & MALAYSIA

FISH HEAD CURRY

Though most Westerners shy away from dishes in which the main ingredient's eyes are included, Singaporeans swear it's the fish's head that contains the sweetest meat in this soupy curry.

METHOD

1 Heat the oil in a large soup pan over a medium heat, add the fenugreek seeds and saute for 1 minute.

2 Add the curry leaves and garlic and saute for another minute.

3 Add the onions and chillies and fry for about 10 minutes, until the onions are light brown.

4 Add the curry powder and fry for another 5 minutes, until fragrant.

5 Add a splash of water and the tamarind paste and salt and bring to a boil.

6 Reduce the heat and simmer for 10 minutes.

7 Add the fish head, okra, tofu, tomatoes, remaining water and coconut milk and simmer until the fish is cooked, about 10 minutes.

8 Turn off the heat and garnish with coriander leaves.

TASTING NOTES

Beautifully combining elements from across the continent, Peranakan fish head curry has a sour-spice flavour that's reminiscent of *tom yum* (Thai seafood soup) and is more liquid than traditional Indian curry. Eschew the Indian hand-to-mouth eating method; you'll want a spoon. The flavour comes from tamarind paste while the spice comes from chillies, the former acting as a brake on the latter, giving this dish a slow burn. Though the fish head is the dish's star, the fried tofu soaks up most of the flavour and okra adds crunch. For extra authenticity – or to impress your friends – try eating an eyeball. They are crunchy on the outside and gooey on the inside! ● *by Joshua Samuel Brown*

ORIGINS

Though chili is a humble food, its origin story is baroquely bizarre. According to legend, the recipe was invented by a 17th-century Spanish nun, Sister Mary of Ágreda, who is said to have gone into trances and teleported to the American West, where she helped to evangelise the Native Americans. Supernatural tales aside, chili was probably invented by poor Texan settlers in the 1800s, who stewed tough chunks of beef into edibility.

TASTING NOTES

Texas chili is a hearty meat-and-chilli stew, distinguished from other types of chili by its lack of beans or tomatoes. Though you can sample it at nearly any greasy-spoon diner in the Lone Star State, attending a cook-off is undoubtedly the most authentic way to taste it. Buy yourself a raffle ticket, grab a spoon, and get ready for some heat. The best chilis will be thick and never greasy, with tender chunks of meat and a slow-smoked flavour. The type of chilli used depends on the cook – popular bets are smoky *guajillos*; rich, dark *pasillas*; or singing-hot *árbols*. Cool your mouth down with a fat wedge of cornbread and a slug of Texas lager. ● *by Emily Matchar*

SERVES 4

USA

FIVE ALARM TEXAS CHILI

In Texas, this slow-simmered beef dish with its fiery
chilli paste is known as a 'bowl o' red'. The more
'alarms', the hotter the chili – five is the maximum.

YOU'LL NEED

500g (1lb) beef mince
1 tbs oil
1 cup (250mL) passata
2 cups (500mL) water
½–2 tsp ground cayenne
  pepper (depending on how
  spicy you want it)
1½ tsp salt
1½ tsp cumin
1½ tsp oregano
1½ tsp paprika
1 small onion, peeled and
  minced
2 cloves of garlic, peeled and
  minced
Grated Cheddar cheese and
  sour cream to serve

METHOD

1 Brown the beef in the oil in a large saucepan over a medium-
high heat.

2 Add the passata and water and stir.

3 Add the remaining ingredients and bring to a simmer.

4 Simmer for 45 minutes, stirring occasionally.

5 Serve with grated Cheddar cheese and sour cream.

ORIGINS

Creative Thai cooks don't like to waste food – so they came up a novel way to involve every part of the fish in the cooking process. By fermenting the fish stomach (and sometimes other organs) they created *tai plaa*, a concoction that is vastly different from the more famous Thai curries and has its own special taste. In Southern Thailand coconut milk is often added to give it a local flavour; upcountry the coconut milk is usually omitted.

YOU'LL NEED

Tai plaa paste
3 tbs fermented fish stomach
Handful of dried chilli pepper
2 tbs cumin
2 tbs sliced galangal
2 cloves of garlic, peeled
1 tbs chopped lemongrass
1 tbs black pepper
1 tbs of kaffir lime rind
2 red onions, peeled
Pinch of salt

Curry
3–4 cups (750mL–1L) of water
1 cup of bamboo shoots
Handful of Thai aubergines, cut into wedges if necessary
Handful of long beans, cut into short lengths
3 kaffir lime leaves
1 tbs of shrimp paste (*gra-bee*)
1 cup of dried fish (tuna, Thai mackerel or saba)
1 tbs lime juice
Boiled rice to serve
1 cucumber, sliced, to serve

SERVES 4

SOUTHERN THAILAND

GAANG TAI PLAA

For an authentic Thai curry that packs a potent punch, this fermented fish dish is a clear winner. Its unique curry paste simply explodes with flavour – and tongue-tingling heat.

METHOD

1 Place the fermented fish stomach in a mortar with the dried chillies. Bash them up with a pestle, then pour in the other *tai plaa* ingredients and blend and bash together.

2 Pour 2 cups (500mL) of the water into a wok and bring to a boil. Stir in the *tai plaa* paste, bamboo shoots, Thai aubergines, long beans, kaffir lime leaves and shrimp paste and pound some more.

3 Add the dried fish with a little lime juice.

4 Let this simmer for around 5 minutes. Add water as needed to reduce saltiness.

5 Serve with boiled rice and a side salad of sliced cucumber.

TASTING NOTES

Chances are you'll be perched on wooden benches with your toes in the sand somewhere in Southern Thailand when you sample the salty brilliance of this curry. Like a good wine, it's worth taking in the powerful aroma first before ladling the *gaang tai plaa* over your rice. Let the curry soak in to the rice before pushing it on to your spoon, Thai-style. Enjoy the meaty fish chunks, the slight crunchiness of eggplant and long beans, and the admiring stares of locals who marvel at your ability to survive their local dish. Unlike other Thai curries, this one isn't simply laden with chillies; the peppers and paste give it an extra layer of heat. ● *by Mark Beales*

YOU'LL NEED

Salad

75g (3oz) bean sprouts
100g (3½oz) green beans, cut
   into 5cm (2in) lengths
200g (7oz) cabbage, sliced
   thinly
250g (9oz) tofu, fried till
   golden, quartered
2 eggs, boiled, quartered
1 medium cucumber,
   quartered lengthways then
   sliced into 3cm (11/4in)
   pieces
2 stalks Chinese celery, finely
   chopped
2 spring onions (scallions),
   finely chopped
20g (1oz) *krupuk* (prawn
   crackers)

Peanut Sauce

2 cloves of garlic, peeled
10 bird's-eye chillies
20g (1oz) *gula melaka* (palm
   sugar)
½ tsp salt
200g (7oz) peanuts, roasted
½ tbs shrimp paste
1 lime, juiced (or equivalent
   tamarind juice)
½ tbs *kecap manis* (sweet soy
   sauce)
1½ cups (375mL) water

Optional

Fried tempeh, sliced into
   bite-size portions

ORIGINS

Many central ingredients in
modern-day Indonesian cooking
– particularly chilli and nuts –
were brought to Indonesia by
the Spanish and Portuguese
around the 16th century. While
nobody can trace the origins
of *gado gado*, it's not hard to
imagine it thrown together with
available seasonal vegetables,
dressed with something spicy.
Indonesian chef William Wongso
says it's 'probably been around
for as long as we've had
nuts and chillies.'

SERVES 4

INDONESIA

GADO GADO

Literally translating as '*mix mix*', this refreshing vegetable, tofu, potato and egg salad dressed with a spicy peanut sauce is the Indonesian street food of choice, eaten throughout the day.

METHOD

1 For the sauce, grind the garlic, chillies, *gula melaka*, salt, peanuts and shrimp paste with a mortar and pestle until coarse. You can blitz this mixture in the food processor if you don't have a mortar and pestle.

2 Transfer the mixture to a bowl. Add the lime juice and *kecap manis* and mix well.

3 Slowly add the water, stirring the mixture at the same time. The sauce should have a gluggy consistency and not be too watery.

4 Prepare your salad by blanching the bean sprouts and green beans until they are cooked but still have crunch.

5 Combine all the salad ingredients in a big mixing bowl. Add the peanut sauce, stir through to coat and serve.

6 Serve the *krupuk* on the side to crumble over the salad just before eating.

TASTING NOTES

There's something authentic about wandering into a *warung* (small, family-run eatery) in Indonesia and not having to decipher a menu in Bahasa Indonesian because it's so easy to say, '*Gado gado satu, terimah kasih*' ('One *gado gado*, thank you'). The salad is a study in texture and a medley of flavours. The base is simultaneously warm (blanched veggies) and cold (fresh vegies), soft yet crunchy and the topping of *krupuk* (fried prawn crackers, a bit like potato chips on steroids) adds a crispy savoury bite. The peanut sauce that binds the dish together has a rich roasted nuttiness that's sweet, sour, spicy and crunchy all at the same time – just try not to lick your plate when you're done. ● *by Shawn Low*

ORIGINS

Thousands of years ago, the culinary tradition known as Xiang arose in response to the hot and humid climates of China's central region. To help sweat it out, fiery Xiang dishes rely on liberal amounts of chilli and garlic cooked in lashings of oil. Though simple, *gan guo* requires mastery to ensure everything is cooked at just the right times and temperatures to bring out flavours.

YOU'LL NEED

Marinade

1 tbs Shaoxing wine
1 tsp light soy sauce
1 tsp dark soy sauce
1 tbs cornflour
Pinch of salt
1 tbs water

Gan guo

340g (12oz) beef
5 tbs peanut oil
1 cup Chinese celery, very finely sliced
6 dried bird's-eye chillies, coarsely chopped
2 tsp dried chilli flakes
2 tsp ground cumin
1 tsp dark soy sauce
2 tsp grated fresh ginger
1 tbs garlic, peeled and finely chopped
1 tsp sesame oil
2 spring onions (scallions), very finely sliced
Salt and pepper to taste

TASTING NOTES

For a full *gan guo* experience you will need one extra ingredient: an unbearably hot day. You'll already be sweating when you perch on your stool at a street stall, ready to dig in. Wait until the sizzling plate quiets, then take a bite. You'll be bowled over by the intensely savoury, sweet and spicy flavours of the beef, the crunch of celery, and the lingering kick of chilli. This is the magic of cooking over fast, high heat; dry-wok cooking drives out the moisture from ingredients without burning them, lending a uniquely crisp and chewy texture. And as the sweat drips down your face and your eyes water, you'll have forgotten all about the scorching weather. ● *by Tienlon Ho*

HUNAN, CHINA

GAN GUO

Dig into the sizzling red chillies of this signature dish from central China to get to the main attraction – beef, cooked *gan guo* or 'dry wok' until caramelised and crisp.

METHOD

1 In a bowl, combine the wine, soy sauces, cornflour, salt and water to make the marinade.

2 Slice the beef across the grain into thin slices, then toss in the marinade.

3 Heat a wok over a high flame until a drop of water evaporates within a second or two of contact. Add 1 tbs of oil, then the celery, chillies, chilli flakes and cumin and stir-fry briefly until fragrant. Transfer the celery to a plate.

4 Add the remaining oil and heat until hot. Drain any excess marinade then add the meat.

5 Cook, undisturbed, for 1 minute, letting the beef begin to sear. Then stir-fry for 1 minute, until the beef starts to release its juices and

pan is sizzling as the liquid evaporates.

6 Reduce the heat to medium and continue stir-frying for a few minutes until the beef is well browned and the wok is almost dry.

7 Swirl the soy sauce into the wok and stir-fry for a few seconds until well combined.

8 Add the ginger and garlic and stir-fry for a few seconds until fragrant.

9 Add the celery again and stir-fry until warmed through and combined.

10 Add the sesame oil and spring onions, then salt and pepper to taste.

11 Remove immediately from the heat and serve.

ORIGINS

The origin of these thin, springy wheat noodles is generally thought to be China. However, down the centuries rāmen has become a cornerstone of Japanese cuisine and there's a vast range of ways to serve the noodles, either in a soupy stock or dry with dipping sauce. In fact, rāmen has developed an international cult following, with chefs vying to prepare unique recipes, including *gekikara*.

YOU'LL NEED

2L (3½ pints) chicken stock
4 garlic cloves, smashed
4cm root ginger, sliced
1 leek, chopped
1 carrot, chopped
1 piece of *kombu*
1 tsp white pepper
2 tbsp soy sauce
2 tbsp mirin (cooking sake)
2 tbsp white sugar
120ml (4oz) *gochujang* paste/ hot pepper paste
1–2 tbsp chilli oil to taste
540g (1lb) ramen noodles, cooked
2 hard boiled eggs, halved pickled bamboo shoots, nori sheets, black sesame seeds and sliced spring onions, to garnish

SERVES 4

JAPAN

GEKIKARA RĀMEN

Gekikara translates from Japanese as 'hellishly spicy'. Slurping these noodles, the broth brimming with chilli and pepper, may be like ingesting molten lava, but is also a curiously addictive experience.

METHOD

1 Add the garlic, ginger, leek, carrot, *kombu* and white pepper to the stock and bring to the boil.

2 Add soy, mirin, sugar, *gochujang* and chilli oil, then reduce the heat and simmer for 15 minutes. Remove the *kombu*, then cook for a further hour. Strain and discard solids.

3 Boil the noodles in plenty of water until *al dente* and divide between four bowls.

4 Top with half an egg, bamboo shoots, nori, sesame seeds and spring onions, then ladle the spicy soup over the top to serve.

TASTING NOTES

Rāmen bars specialising in this dish often make it available in gradations of spiciness, from temporarily tongue numbing to off the radioactive scale. The chef will freshly prepare the dish for you, ladling the fiery red stock, perhaps with an extra dash of chilli oil or generous dose of pepper powder, over the noodles. Then it'll be topped with garnishes such as beansprouts, julienned spring onions, boiled egg and slices of pork. Follow fellow diners by slurping the rāmen noisily while eating, with napkin at the ready to dab your perspiring brow. Despite the feeling of a volcano about to erupt in your belly, don't linger over your bowl: rāmen is eat-and-go food of the fastest order. ● *by Simon Richmond*

YOU'LL NEED

Marinade
3 tsp light soy sauce
2 tsp Shaoxing wine
2 chicken breasts, diced into
　1cm (½in) cubes

Sauce
1 tsp dark soy sauce
1 tsp light soy sauce
3 tsp Chinese black vinegar
1 tsp sesame oil
1 tbs water
2 tsp sugar
A pinch of cornflour

Stir-fry
12 dried red chillies
4 tbs oil
2 tsp whole Sichuan
　peppercorns
3cm (1¼in) piece of fresh
　ginger, peeled and thinly
　sliced
3 cloves of garlic, peeled and
　thinly sliced
3 spring onions (scallions), cut
　into 2cm (¾in) pieces
⅔ cup plain roasted peanuts

ORIGINS
The dish is named after Ding
Baozhen, a Qing-era bureaucrat
whose title was Gong Bao. While
Ding was ruling Shandong, he
crossed paths with eunuch and
rumoured lover of the Empress
Dowager, who was forbidden
under pain of beheading from
leaving Peking. Ding executed
the protégé and put his body on
display to reveal his castration
and save the Empress Dowager's
reputation. Ding became
governor of Sichuan, where he is
said to have invented the dish.

SERVES 2

SICHUAN, CHINA

GONG BAO CHICKEN

A fiery dance of chicken and peanuts, with a kick of dried chillies and a flourish of Sichuan pepper. Tamer versions abound, but it's most tantalising in its authentic form.

METHOD

1 Mix together the light soy sauce and the Shaoxing wine to make the marinade. Pour it over the chicken, toss to coat evenly and marinade for 2 hours.

2 Mix together all the sauce ingredients.

3 Snip off the stems of the chillies. Leave the chillies whole if you want the dish to be really hot. If not, half them and remove the seeds.

4 Pour the oil into a wok or pan. When it is hot add the chillies and Sichuan pepper and stir-fry quickly for a few seconds until fragrant, taking care not to let it burn.

5 Add the chicken and its marinade, ginger, garlic and spring onions, and continue to stir-fry until the meat is just cooked.

6 Pour the sauce into the wok or pan, stirring and tossing to coat the ingredients thoroughly. As soon as the sauce becomes thick add the peanuts.

7 Serve immediately.

TASTING NOTES

The dish is characterised by *ma-la* or 'hot and numbing' spiciness unique to Sichuan. The *la* (heat) comes from the dried chillies while the aromatic dark-pink Sichuan peppercorns, known as 'flower pepper' in Chinese, provide the *ma* (numbing feeling). It's the contrast of chicken and peanuts that excites the palate – tender, succulent subtlety versus dry, crunchy roundedness. As you chew, the complex *ma-la* flavours in the oil are released and build up slowly into a tingling wave of heat. If you like chillies, the seared dried chillies pack a punch. The peppercorns, though deliciously aromatic, are better left alone. The dish is perfect with a bowl of fluffy white rice. ● *by Piera Chen*

YOU'LL NEED

1 tbs vegetable oil

2 medium onions, peeled and diced

500g (1lb) stewing or braising beef, cubed

2 cloves of garlic, peeled and minced

3 tbs Hungarian paprika

1 tsp caraway seeds, ground

Pinch of cayenne pepper

2–3 cups (500–750mL) of water

400g (14oz) potatoes, peeled and cubed

3 medium carrots, peeled and cubed

Salt to taste

Crusty bread or fresh egg noodles to serve

ORIGINS

Goulash was the staple meal of herders who drove cattle on Hungary's plains as far back as the 9th century. The herdsmen would cook the stew in iron kettles over a fire, supposedly using animals that couldn't make the trip, until it was almost dry so it could be stored in sheep's-stomach bags and later reconstituted with water. Paprika was not considered a crucial ingredient until the Turks introduced the spice to the country in the 18th century.

HUNGARY

GOULASH

Hungary's national dish – a hearty feast of tender beef chunks and root vegetables flavoured with local paprika – has been sustaining everyone from Magyar cattle-herders to restaurant-goers for generations.

METHOD

1 Heat the oil in a heavy-based casserole pot. Add the onions and cook until soft and golden.

2 Add the beef and stir-fry until the meat is no longer pink and any liquid has evaporated.

3 Add the garlic, paprika, caraway seeds and cayenne pepper and fry for a few minutes to coat the beef. Add enough water to just cover the meat. Bring to a boil.

4 Add the potatoes and carrots.

5 Turn down the heat to a simmer and cook

the goulash for at least an hour or until the beef is tender and the potatoes and carrots are cooked.

6 Season the soup with salt and more caraway as required.

7 Serve with crusty bread or fresh egg noodles.

TIP *An easy dish to replicate at home but do try to use Hungarian paprika, which gives the dish its characteristic warmth and bittersweet taste. Chop the meat and vegetables to the same approximate sizes for even cooking.*

TASTING NOTES

Long, cold winters in Hungary require nourishing slow-cooked foods such as goulash, which goes perfectly with noodles or dumplings. Not to be confused with that other Hungarian staple *pörkölt* (a dry-fried meat stew), a bowl of goulash is a one-pot wonder of beef and vegetables that becomes a complete meal when cooked with egg noodles called *csipetke*. Unlike the smoky Spanish version or the mild, generic versions found in most supermarkets, the Hungarian paprika lends an intense red-capsicum flavour and deep-red colour to the dish. It comes in mild, sweet, semisweet and hot varieties, depending on the type of capsicum, but even the hot versions will have a more complex aroma and taste than cayenne or chilli powder. ● *by Johanna Ashby*

BRIAN D CRUICKSHANK © GETTY IMAGES

ORIGINS

In legend, the soup first appeared in 1600s West Africa after Spanish and Portuguese colonists brought groundnuts from South America. The nuts were an ideal thickener when dairy products were difficult to obtain. Today, African-Americans often serve peanut butter soup during the holiday of Kwanzaa between December 26 and January 1 to celebrate the nut's tie to their African roots.

YOU'LL NEED

1 whole chicken, jointed, preferably free range and corn fed
2 medium onions, peeled
Salt to taste
1 large, very ripe tomato
1 Scotch bonnet chilli pepper
Pinch cayenne pepper
3cm (1¼in) piece of ginger, peeled and grated
3 tbs peanut butter
1 small glass of water
Additional water
Omo tuo (rice balls) or *fufu* (pounded cassava) to serve

TASTING NOTES

You're not looking for a bowl of liquid peanut butter; the best groundnut soup is an exercise in subtle nuttiness – deep, rich and enhanced by the zing of Scotch bonnet chillies and an aromatic, tomatoey base. The texture should be silky smooth without descending into sauce-like thickness. Then there's the business of mopping up. Some prefer the dense stickiness of *omo tuo* (balls of pudding rice); others a doughy glob of *fufu* (pounded cassava). Chicken pieces should be firm and on the bone – all the better for dunking and slurping. And forget about cutlery – using your hands is all part of the experience (eat with your right hand please!). ● *by Nana Luckham*

SERVES 4

GHANA

GROUNDNUT SOUP

This spicy soup is traditionally made with roasted groundnuts (peanuts) although peanut butter is commonly used today. Flavoured with ginger, garlic, tomato and chicken, it's your lip-smacking passport to West Africa.

METHOD

1 Put the chicken pieces in a large pot, cast iron if possible.

2 Chop one of the onions and scatter over the chicken along with a pinch of salt.

3 Put the pan on the lowest heat, cover and cook very gently for 15 minutes.

4 Don't chop the remaining onion, the tomato or the Scotch bonnet chilli pepper; instead keep them whole and add them to the pot with the cayenne pepper and grated ginger, then cook gently for 10 more minutes.

5 Meanwhile put the peanut butter in a blender along with the glass of water and whizz to a smooth paste.

6 Pour the peanut paste into the pot and simmer for 10 minutes.

7 Remove the tomato, onion and Scotch bonnet chilli pepper from the pan. Put them in the blender and puree to a smooth paste.

8 Transfer the paste back into the pot, add enough water to just cover the chicken and simmer for 30 minutes. Serve with *omo tuo* or *fufu*.

ORIGINS

You'll find 'beef noodle soup' throughout Asia, but Taiwan has made this dish its own by localising the ingredients and spicing it up several notches. Beef consumption wasn't big here before 1949 so it's likely the recipe was brought to the island by mainlanders fleeing China's civil war. Spicy stewed-beef noodle soup has existed in China since the Tang Dynasty (AD 618–906). It was popularised by members of the Hui, a Chinese Muslim ethnic group known for hand-pulled noodles.

YOU'LL NEED

1kg (2lb) beef chuck roast, cut into 4 chunks

Salt

3 tbs canola oil

1 tsp Chinese five spice powder

8 cloves of garlic, finely chopped

2cm (¾in) piece of fresh ginger, sliced

5 spring onions (scallions), cut crosswise

4 dried star anise

2–4 tbs Sichuan peppercorns

3–4 red chillies, split lengthwise

¼ cup (60mL) chilli bean sauce

¼ cup (60mL) rice wine

6 tbs light soy sauce

2 tbs dark soy sauce

5 cups (1¼L) water

1 bok choy cut into large chunks

500g (1lb) thick Chinese egg noodles

SERVES 6

TAIWAN

HONG SHAO NIU ROU MIAN

A feature on the Asian-must visit culinary map, Taiwanese dishes aren't generally renowned for their incendiary spiciness. This slow-cooked pot of blistering beefy broth with noodles may just change that.

METHOD

1 Season the beef with salt. Heat the oil in a pot, add the beef and sear it on both sides.

2 Add all remaining soup ingredients, except for the bok choy and noodles. Bring to a boil, skimming fat from the top as necessary. Lower the heat and simmer for about 2 hours.

3 Take the soup off the heat and uncover the pot to allow the steam to evaporate and the broth to become more concentrated as it cools.

4 When the broth has cooled, remove the meat and set it aside.

5 Strain the broth into another pot, discarding any solids, then reheat the broth over a medium heat.

6 Cut the meat into 1cm- (1/2in-) thick pieces before returning it to broth. Add the bok choy.

7 Cook the noodles in separate pot of water until cooked to the desired texture. Strain and place in individual bowls.

8 Ladle over the broth, meat and bok choy.

TASTING NOTES

So readily available is this dish in Taiwan that most take its complexity for granted; but as any chef will attest, making good spicy beef noodle soup is complex and time-consuming. Is it worth it? Yes! The secret lies in the process of heating and cooling, allowing the broth to concentrate a very diverse list of ingredients into a unified, spicy – and uniquely Taiwanese – flavour. Good spicy beef noodle soup tempts the tongue without burning it, the anise and five spice offering a rich, savoury counterpoint to the fiery Sichuanese chillies. The beef is flavoursome and tender enough to pull apart with chopsticks, and is often served with chilli-infused dark vinegar mixed with soy sauce. ● *by Joshua Samuel Brown*

ORIGINS

Scottish immigrants settling in the American South brought with them a taste for fried food. Later, slave cooks on plantations added their spices. The 'hot' twist comes from Nashville's Prince's Hot Chicken restaurant. Supposedly, the original owner's girlfriend secretly doused his chicken in pepper as revenge for cheating. He loved it so much he opened a restaurant specialising in the mouth-burning stuff!

YOU'LL NEED

8 cups (2L) cold water
1 cup (250mL) hot sauce (such as Tabasco)
150g (5oz) plus 1 tsp salt
100g (3½oz) plus ½ tsp sugar
1.6–1.8kg (3½–4lb) whole chicken, quartered
11 cups (2.8L) peanut oil
1 tbs cayenne pepper
½ tsp paprika
¼ tsp garlic powder
250g (9oz) flour
Black pepper to taste
Sliced white bread and sliced pickles to serve

TASTING NOTES

Sampling hot chicken requires patience. The best of the Nashville establishments specialising in the dish use cast-iron pans to fry their chicken, which takes significantly longer than using a deep-fryer. Order a white-meat breast quarter, or – the local preference – a dark-meat thigh quarter, and choose from mild, medium, hot or extra hot. Newbies shouldn't be embarrassed to go mild – believe us, it will be more humiliating to spit out a bite of extra hot when you discover you can't take the nuclear heat. The crispy skin is orange with chilli, dripping flavoursome juice from the brined meat. If the heat is getting to you, order extra slices of cottony white bread to cool down your tongue. ● *by Emily Matchar*

SERVES 4

NASHVILLE, TENNESSEE, USA

HOT CHICKEN

In Nashville, 'hot' chicken doesn't describe temperature, it refers to the near-atomic spice level of this chilli-battered delight, served with bread and pickle chips at hole-in-the-wall restaurants throughout Music City.

METHOD

1 In a large bowl, stir the cold water, hot sauce, 150g salt and 100g sugar until the salt and sugar dissolve. Add the chicken and refrigerate, covered, for 30 minutes.

2 Preheat the oven to 195°C (200°F).

3 Heat 3 tbs oil in a small saucepan over medium heat, and add the cayenne, paprika, garlic powder, ½ tsp salt and remaining sugar. Cook for 30 seconds then transfer to a small bowl.

4 Remove the chicken from refrigerator and pour off the brine.

5 In a large bowl, combine the flour, remaining salt and black pepper to taste.

6 Dredge the chicken pieces in the flour

mixture then shake off any excess. Repeat, then transfer the chicken to a wire rack.

7 In a large Dutch oven over medium-high heat, heat the remaining oil to 175°C (350°F).

8 Fry the chicken, two pieces at a time, at 150–160°C (300–325°F) until the skin is golden brown (about 30 minutes). White meat must register 70°C (160°F) and dark meat 80°C (175°F).

9 Drain on a wire rack and keep warm in a preheated oven while cooking the remaining chicken pieces.

10 Stir the spicy oil to recombine and brush over the chicken. Serve sliced white bread with sliced pickles.

ORIGINS

Like many Caribbean dishes, Jamaican jerk traces its roots back to West Africa, where meats were spiced with a variety of tasty, tongue-numbing spices prior to cooking. There are two prevailing theories on the origin of the term jerk – one says it comes from the Spanish word *charqui*, meaning dried meat. Most Jamaicans, however, insist the term jerk comes from the cooking method, which calls for regular turning (or jerking, in Jamaica).

TASTING NOTES

Good jerk should be simultaneously spicy and sweet, paradoxically simple and complex; the sweetness of molasses brings out the fiery habañero peppers (not for the faint of heart) without masking them, while the hodge-podge of other Caribbean spices adds a veritable bouquet of flavours not found in a typical barbecue dish. The meat, marinated for at least four hours, is tender enough to cut with a spoon. But making it is more art than science, and a true jerk chef cooks as much from intuition as any set recipe. When cooking your own, turn and baste frequently to keep the meat from drying out. Leftover marinade can be boiled (to sterilise it) and used for dipping sauce. ● *by Joshua Samuel Brown*

SERVES 4

CARIBBEAN

JAMAICAN JERK

Jerk refers to both a spice mix and a cooking method: the marinade redolent with allspice, cloves, nutmeg, cinnamon and thyme and the chicken 'jerked' frequently over a hot flame.

YOU'LL NEED

1 tbs ground allspice
1 tbs dried thyme
½ tsp cayenne pepper
½ tsp freshly ground black pepper
½ tsp ground sage
¾ tsp ground nutmeg
¾ tsp ground cinnamon
2 tbs garlic powder
1 tbs molasses
¼ cup (60mL) olive oil
¼ cup (60mL) soy sauce
¾ cup (180mL) apple cider vinegar
½ cup (125mL) orange juice
2 habañero peppers, finely chopped
3 green onions, peeled and finely chopped
2–3kg (4–6¼lb) chicken breasts

METHOD

1 Create the marinade by combining all of the ingredients above in a large bowl. Cover, place in the refrigerator and leave the chicken to marinate overnight.

2 When you are ready to cook, lift out the chicken pieces and cook under a medium-high grill or on a barbecue, turning and basting frequently.

ORIGINS

The word jambalaya is said to combine the French word for ham (*jambon*) with *à la* (meaning 'with') and *ya*, a West African word for rice, though this may be apocryphal. Born in Cajun Country Louisiana, it was probably an attempt to make paella without saffron. Local cooks substituted tomatoes for colour and flavour, and the dish became popular among frugal home cooks looking to make a hearty meal with whatever odds and ends were in the house.

LOUISIANA, USA

JAMBALAYA

Iconic enough to inspire a classic country song (Hank Williams' 'Jambalaya (On the Bayou)'), jambalaya is the original fusion cuisine, a rice and meat concoction with a thousand possible variations.

YOU'LL NEED

2 tsp olive oil
2 boneless chicken breasts, chopped into 2.5cm (1in) pieces
250g (9oz) Andouille sausage, sliced
1 onion, peeled and diced
1 capsicum (bell pepper), diced
1 stick celery, diced
2 cloves of garlic, peeled and chopped
½–1 tsp cayenne pepper
½ tsp onion powder
Salt and pepper to taste
400g (14oz) white rice
4 cups (1L) chicken stock
3 bay leaves
2 tsp Worcestershire sauce
1 tsp hot sauce (such as Tabasco)

METHOD

1 In a large saucepan, heat the oil over medium-high heat. Saute chicken and Andouille sausage until lightly browned.

2 Add the onion, capsicum, celery, garlic, cayenne, onion powder and salt and pepper.

3 Cook, stirring, until the onions are soft and translucent, about 5 minutes.

4 Add the rice, chicken stock and bay leaves. Bring to the boil, then reduce the heat, cover and simmer for 20 minutes.

5 Stir in the Worcestershire sauce and hot sauce and serve.

TASTING NOTES

Jambalaya is best known as a home-cooked dish, a staple of family Sunday lunches or church picnics. And everyone's grandmère makes the best version, mais oui! Non-natives can seek jambalaya at the more casual – some might say divey – pubs and late-night haunts of New Orleans. Order a steaming bowl of whatever's on special that night – gamey rabbit, salty-savoury sausage, sweet crayfish – and chow down, shaking more vinegary Louisiana hot sauce on to taste. Each bite holds dozens of flavours – the freshness of rice, the meaty chew of Andouille, the sting of garlic, the brininess of shrimp. Cool your sizzling taste buds with a chilled Abita ale, brewed just 30 miles away from NoLa. ● *by Emily Matchar*

ORIGINS

Rumour has it that jollof rice was first cooked up by members of the Wolof tribe in Senegal (Wolof/jollof, get it?), whose empire covered wide swathes of western Africa from the 14th through to the 19th centuries. In some areas, including Gambia, jollof rice is known as *benachin*, which translates as 'one pot'. Whether you add okra, plantain or fish comes down to fiercely held regional preferences. Whatever, the colour remains the same: a joyful bright umber.

YOU'LL NEED

1 tbs olive or vegetable oil

1 large onion, peeled and finely diced

6 large tomatoes, skinned and diced

1 red pepper, finely chopped

1 Scotch bonnet chilli, finely chopped

1 clove garlic, peeled and finely chopped

1 tsp curry powder

2 tbs tomato puree

Salt and freshly ground black pepper

¼ tsp cayenne pepper or chilli powder

225g (8oz) long-grain or basmati rice

1 vegetable or chicken stock cube

2 cups (500mL) boiling water

SERVES 2

WEST AFRICA

JOLLOF RICE

No social function is complete without jollof rice, the poster food for West Africa, a one-pot meal of chilli-spiked rice with tomatoes, onion and a hodge-podge of meat or vegetables.

METHOD

1 Heat the oil in a large pan and cook the onion over a gentle heat until soft.

2 Stir in the tomatoes, red pepper, Scotch bonnet chilli, garlic, curry powder and tomato puree, then season with salt, freshly ground black pepper and the cayenne pepper or chilli powder. Fry for 15 minutes or until you have a thick pulp.

3 Add the rice and fry in the tomato mixture for 1–2 minutes until well coated.

4 Dissolve the stock cube in the water and add the stock to the pan.

5 Bring to the boil then turn to a low heat and simmer, covered, for 20–30 minutes until all the stock is absorbed and the rice is cooked al dente.

6 Serve with fried plantains or alongside grilled meat or fish. To get the right texture, make sure to use long-grain, preferably basmati rice, and don't overdo it on the liquid or you'll end up with a pile of mush.

TASTING NOTES

Good jollof rice isn't going to make you cry chilli-induced tears. It's much more subtle than that – a gentle burn of tomatoes, onions, hot pepper and al-dente rice that builds up slowly enough to warm the taste buds without blowing your head off with intense heat. The best jollof is cooked outdoors in vast iron cauldrons over wood fires, infusing the rice with a delicate smokiness and leaving crunchy scrapings at the bottom of the pan. Eat it in a street-side 'chop bar' (local cafe, often in a shack) to add to the authenticity. Come late morning for lunch or dusk before the evening rush, when the food is fresh, the company warm and the radio blaring. ● *by Nana Luckham*

YOU'LL NEED

7 tomatoes, whole
225g (8oz) tomatillos, whole
3 medium red peppers,
   seeded and roughly
   chopped
1 onion, peeled and roughly
   chopped
1 *guaque* chilli
1 *pasilla* chilli
6 Cobán chillies
6 cloves of garlic, peeled
4 cups (1L) chicken stock
1 tbs annatto-seed paste
1.5kg (3½lb) turkey legs
   (approx 3)
Salt and pepper
1 bunch of spring onion stalks
1 bunch of fresh coriander
   (cilantro), chopped
Handful of mint leaves,
   chopped to garnish

ORIGINS

Kak'ik is the dish time forgot:
unchanged from when the
Q'eqchi' Maya, Guatemala's
largest ethnic group, were
cooking it a millennia back.
Several ingredients, like the
tomatillos and the *guaque/
pasilla* chillies, herald from
the Mexican part of Mayan
civilisation, but true *kak'ik*
concocted in its home (Alta
Verapaz's capital, Cobán) utilises
smoky *chiles cobaneros*
(Cobán chillies).

GUATEMALA

KAK'IK

This ancestral Mayan turkey, tomatillo and annatto-seed soup is as faithful to pre-Hispanic Latin American cuisine as it gets, the startling red hue evoking the blood of ancient sacrificial rites.

METHOD

1 To make the red sauce: place the tomatoes, tomatillos, red peppers, onion, four cloves of garlic, and the *guaque, pasilla* and Cobán chillies under a hot grill. Cook the vegetables until brown and beginning to char.

2 Blend the browned vegetables and the chillies, thinning the mixture if necessary with a little chicken stock (¼ cup or 60mL). Add the annatto-seed paste and blend again. Strain and set to one side.

3 Put the turkey legs in a pot with enough chicken stock to cover each leg. Add one teaspoon of salt and the remaining two garlic cloves.

4 Cover and cook for about 1 hour on a low-medium heat until the turkey is tender.

5 Add the spring onions and half the coriander to the pot after 30 minutes.

6 When the turkey is cooked, remove the spring onions and add the red sauce. Stir well.

7 Add the rest of the chopped coriander and bring slowly to the boil. Reduce the heat to low-medium, and cook for another 30 minutes.

8 Season as desired with salt and pepper. Add mint to garnish.

TASTING NOTES

Visit the rudimentary back-street Mayan kitchens and street-side stalls for the very best *kak'ik*. Preparation begins with the traditional killing, smoking, boiling and plucking of the turkey. Then there's the assembly of the vegetables: the reds (peppers, tomatoes), the greens (tomatillos) and a rainbow of chillies. Cobbled together, the resulting broth should be russet red-orange, achieved by slow roasting and the addition of annatto-seed paste. *Kak'ik* is as hot as its colour suggests. The 'ik' (spiciness) hits you in a four-flanked attack of the three chillies followed by the pepperiness of the annatto seeds, complementing the citrus tang of the tomatillos. A broth is velvety, with the turkey leg falling off your spoon in softened tomato and chilli-infused morsels. ● *by Luke Waterson*

SERVES 6

YOU'LL NEED

500g (1lb) lamb or mutton (cut into 2cm/¾in chunks)
1 tbs sunflower oil
3 tbs ground chilli flakes
3 tbs ground cumin
Sea salt
3 tbs ground black pepper
Skewers (wooden or metal; if using wooden skewers soak in water first so they don't burn on the grill)

ORIGINS

The kebab originated in the eastern Mediterranean millennia ago. The ancient Greeks skewered meats and cooked them over coals, apparently due to a shortage of firewood. Legend has it that Persian soldiers did the same, grilling meat on their swords. Carrying this tradition east to the Uyghurs of Kashgar and across China, they took kebabs to punters from Shanghai to Sichuan, known here as *yangrou chuan* (lamb meat kebabs).

MAKES 12
KEBABS

KASHGAR, XINJIANG, CHINA

KASHGAR LAMB KEBABS

A tangy take on the traditional kebab, these are the quintessential spicy Central Asian street snack: sizzling skewered lamb crusted with chilli, pepper and cumin, cooked over glowing coals.

METHOD

1 Remove the lamb from the refrigerator; these kebabs cook best if the meat is at room temperature prior to cooking. Preheat the barbecue or grill.

2 In a bowl, mix the sunflower oil, chilli flakes, cumin, salt and pepper. The mix will be quite gritty.

3 Thread five or six chunks of lamb on to each skewer.

4 Brush each skewer with the oil and spice mix, ensuring all of them are well lubricated.

5 Place each skewer on to the grill, turning only once and brushing with extra oil and spice mix if desired. The kebabs are ready after about 2 minutes on each side, or when the exterior of the meat is golden-brown with a slight crust of spice.

6 Serve the kebabs with flatbread or rice, and garnish with extra chilli flakes or salt to taste.

TASTING NOTES

Prepare for a sensory surround-sound experience. You'll notice the sound and scent of the kebab stall first: the aroma of the blue smoke rising from the grill, the sizzle of muttony fat dropping on charcoal embers. Stepping up to take your turn, you'll find your hunger mounting and your patience waning in anticipation of the moment when you'll pull the chunks of spicy lamb off with your teeth. The exterior of each morsel is crisp and crusted with salt and chilli flakes: a sharp peppery rebuke. But chewing releases the pungency of moist lamb, an almost sweet rejoinder to counteract the fire. The flavour of the meat is at its height when piping hot, so don't hold back. ● *by Will Gourlay*

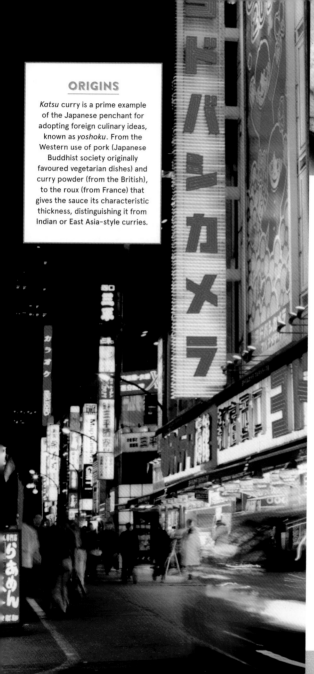

ORIGINS

Katsu curry is a prime example of the Japanese penchant for adopting foreign culinary ideas, known as *yoshoku*. From the Western use of pork (Japanese Buddhist society originally favoured vegetarian dishes) and curry powder (from the British), to the roux (from France) that gives the sauce its characteristic thickness, distinguishing it from Indian or East Asia-style curries.

YOU'LL NEED

Curry Sauce

1 tsp cumin seeds, ground
1 tsp coriander seeds, ground
1 tsp fennel seeds, ground
1 tsp turmeric, ground
1 tbs curry powder
1 tbs vegetable oil
1 medium onion, peeled and diced
1 tbs honey
2 tbs soy sauce
1 tbs rice flour or plain flour dissolved in 2 tbs of water

Pork Cutlet

4 pieces pork loin (approx 500g/1lb)
250g (9oz) Japanese panko or ordinary breadcrumbs
1 large egg, beaten
Plain flour for dusting
Oil for frying

To Serve

Plain boiled rice
Finely shredded cabbage

SERVES 4

JAPAN

KATSU CURRY

Second only to ramen as Japan's favourite food, *katsu* curry is a complete meal of pork cutlet doused with curry sauce served with rice and a side of shredded cabbage.

METHOD

1 Prepare the pork cutlet by flattening each with the back of a knife or a rolling pin to tenderise the meat.

2 Dust each cutlet with flour, dip in the beaten egg then coat with the breadcrumbs. Refrigerate for at least half an hour.

3 To make the curry sauce, dry-fry the spices and curry powder in a saucepan for a few minutes to release their aromas, then add the oil, onion, honey and soy sauce and cook for a few minutes until the onions have softened.

4 Add the flour mixture and cook until the sauce has thickened. Set aside.

5 To cook the pork cutlets, fry them in a pan with oil over medium heat, being careful not to overcrowd the pan. Cook both sides of each cutlet until the crumbs are golden. Drain the cooked cutlets on a wire rack or paper towel.

6 Serve the pork cutlets with plain boiled rice, topped with the curry sauce and garnished with the shredded cabbage.

TASTING NOTES

It might seem like a bit of a production line, buying a meal ticket from a vending machine and queueing up for seats at one of Japan's curry houses, which are likely to serve only one type of *katsu* curry and have their own cult following. Crisp and juicy deep-fried pork cutlets served with gooey, mildly sweet but still pungent curry, rice to soak up the sauce and balance the crunch, and raw shredded cabbage to refresh the palate, make for a satisfying meal. Despite its richness, the Japanese enjoy *katsu* curry just as much in the summer as winter, believing spicy foods to be good for stimulating the appetite, washing it down with an ice-cold beer or soft drink. ● *by Johanna Ashby*

YOU'LL NEED

2–3 cups vegetable oil, plus
    2 tbs, for frying
2½ tbs red curry paste
1 tsp curry powder
½ tsp ground turmeric
1 tsp ground cardamom
    (optional)
3 cups unsweetened coconut
    milk
1½–2kg (3–4lb) chicken, cut
    into 6 pieces
1¾ cups chicken stock
1 tsp sugar
2 tbs fish sauce, or more to
    taste
700g (1½lb) fresh egg noodles
    or 350g (¾lb) dried
2–6 dried red chillies
⅓ cup shallots, thinly sliced
¾ cup Chinese pickled
    mustard greens, chopped
1 lime, cut into wedges
handful coriander leaves
    (cilantro), chopped
⅓ cup spring onions, chopped

ORIGINS

Khao soi is thought to have
roots in Myanmar (Burma),
where Chinese Muslims from
Yunnan province brought an
early version down to Thailand
and Laos. Originally said to be
halal (so, pork free), it now can
contain pork, as well as the
more usual beef and chicken.
Curry paste was added later,
along with coconut milk, to
create a rich, reasonably spicy
dish that is enjoyed mainly in the
afternoon and evening.

TASTING NOTES

If you're lucky, the noodles might still be made manually, with the wheat ground, boiled,
stretched and sliced by hand. What you want in the dish is balance: spice, but not so much
it overpowers; coconut milk, added in just the right amount so it doesn't overwhelm and
make everything dull and overly sweet. The meat should be cooked in the broth, the noodles
soft and chewy. The deep-fried noodles on top should shatter between the teeth. Oh, and
that pickled cabbage is essential: it adds a welcome sour note, along with the lime. Sit down
at the rickety table, and slurp and sip to your heart's content. *Khao soi* satisfies every
eating urge. ● *by Tom Parker Bowles*

NORTHERN THAILAND

KHAO SOI

Chiang Mai's signature dish is a creamy, spicy Thai comfort curry with noodles two ways and a side order of zesty pickled cabbage.

METHOD

1 Heat 2 tbs of the oil in a large, heavy saucepan over medium heat then add the red curry paste, curry powder, turmeric and optional cardamom. Cook, stirring constantly for about two minutes.

2 Add one cup of the coconut milk and bring to a boil, stirring well for about two minutes. Add one more cup of coconut milk, return to a boil, and again boil for about two minutes.

3 Add the chicken pieces, one cup of chicken stock and remaining coconut milk then bring to a boil again. Simmer and thin the broth as needed with chicken stock or water.

4 Add the sugar and fish sauce. Cover and simmer for about 45 minutes.

5 If you're using dried noodles, cook all the noodles in a large pot of boiling water, stirring well till they are tender but firm, about seven minutes or more. If you're using fresh noodles, set aside one cup, then boil the rest till tender and firm, about three minutes. Drain and rinse well in cold water then add a dash of oil and mix well to prevent the noodles from sticking together. If you used dried noodles, set aside one cup of the noodles and dry them with a clean dishtowel.

6 Heat the remaining oil in a large saucepan over medium-high heat. Place the cup of towel-dried noodles or the cup of uncooked fresh noodles into the saucepan a few strands at a time. Fry them, turning once, until crisp and golden. Remove from the heat and set aside. Add the dried chillies to the pan and fry for a few seconds until they puff up; set aside.

7 Divide the remaining boiled noodles into four bowls. Ladle the chicken curry over the noodles and top with shallots, mustard greens, fried noodles, lime wedges, fried chillies, coriander leaves and spring onion, and serve.

YOU'LL NEED

1 tbs sesame oil

300g (11oz) pork, preferably pork rashers or pork belly, chopped

About 2 cups (500mL) of *kimchi* – the older and funkier the better

½ onion, peeled and sliced

3 cloves of garlic, peeled and crushed

2 tbs *gochujang* (hot pepper paste)

3 cups (750mL) hot water

200g (7oz) tofu, chopped

¼ cup chopped spring onions (scallions)

Steamed rice to serve

ORIGINS

Despite being built to last, even *kimchi* can pass its best, but that doesn't mean it's ready for retirement. *Kimchi jjigae* was designed with recycling in mind using leftover *kimchi*. The stew is ideal on crisp, cold days and is being prescribed (non-medically of course) to clear up colds. Despite its heat – both of the temperature and spice varieties – you'll find it on menus nationwide even in the steamiest summer months.

SERVES 4

KOREA

KIMCHI JJIGAE

This fiery stew features the country's most famous ingredient, *kimchi*, boiled up with scallions, onion, garlic and *gochujang* (red pepper paste), and topped off with pork, tofu or tinned tuna.

METHOD

1 Heat a deep saucepan, add the sesame oil and heat briefly.

2 Add the pork and fry until lightly browned and any fat is slightly crispy.

3 Add the *kimchi* and cook for 2 minutes, stirring occasionally.

4 Add the sliced onion, crushed or minced garlic and two generous dollops of *gochujang* (more if your spice threshold is higher!)

5 Add 2 cups (500mL) of the water, plus any juices from the *kimchi* and bring to the boil.

6 Partially remove the lid and reduce the heat, simmering for 20–30 minutes. Add more water if the broth begins to evaporate or is too pungent for your tastes.

7 Add the chopped tofu and simmer for a further 10 minutes.

8 Sprinkle on the chopped scallions just before you remove the stew from the heat, and stir.

9 Serve the stew with steamed rice on the side – and keep a handkerchief handy!

TASTING NOTES

Like many of the country's stews, *kimchi jjigae* is served literally boiling hot, the broth still bubbling when it reaches your table. It's traditionally a communal dish, and while you'll often find it surrounded by the numerous *banchan* (side dishes) ubiquitous in Korean cuisine, it can also be ordered as a main meal with a simple side of rice at inexpensive lunchtime eateries. Stewed *kimchi* retains a touch of crunch and lends a complex flavour to the broth – you'll taste not only the ingredients added to the pot but also everything used to make the *kimchi* itself. To soften the heat, eat it with a little rice, or keep a stash of plain rice aside to chomp between slurps. ● *by Lucy Corne*

ORIGINS

Klobasa's beginnings are unclear, but the Slovenian story goes that it became popular during the times of the Austro-Hungarian empire in the early 19th century. Reputedly it was first crafted in the Gorenjska region of what is now modern Slovenia, from where butchers in Trzin supplied markets across the empire. Today, you can order *klobasa* from a late-night sausage stand or in a Slovenian, Czech or Slovak pub, along with mandatory glass of *pivo* (beer).

CENTRAL EUROPE

KLOBASA

Served with a beer, *klobasa's* mix of smoked pork sausage, chilli heat and paprika sweetness is hard to beat – especially when you crank up the fire with zesty condiments.

YOU'LL NEED

2.5kg (5lb) ground pork
4 cloves of garlic, peeled and crushed
1 medium onion, peeled and finely chopped
1 cup (250mL) white wine
1 tbs ground black pepper
1 tsp caraway seeds
2 tsp salt
4 tsp paprika
1 tsp chilli powder
Sausage casings

METHOD

1 Mix the ground pork together with all the other ingredients. Cover and place in a refrigerator overnight for the flavours to meld.

2 Mix by hand again and fry a small sample to ensure the flavour and seasonings are to your taste.

3 Carefully fill the sausage casings with the meat mixture, squeezing gently to remove any pockets of air.

4 Twist the casings into uniform lengths of about 20cm (8in) long. You should make about 20 sausages.

5 The fresh sausages can then fried, grilled or baked until done, or slowly smoked for around 48 hours.

TASTING NOTES

Don't expect fine dining. You'll probably be served by a gruff barman who is more interested in the ice hockey or football playing on the big-screen TV. If you're ordering *klobasa* in the early hours of the morning from a sausage stand, the proprietor will also be juggling a few servings of fried cheese. But after a big night out, a grilled smoked sausage will be just what you need. There's plenty of heat in the sausage itself – and the sweetish hit of paprika – but the addition of zingy mustard and finely grated fresh horseradish take the culinary punch to another level. To balance it out, you'll also need a slice of caraway-seed infused rye bread. ● *by Brett Atkinson*

FRANCESCO IACOBELLI MILANFOTO, ALEXANDER KLEIN/AFP © GETTY IMAGES

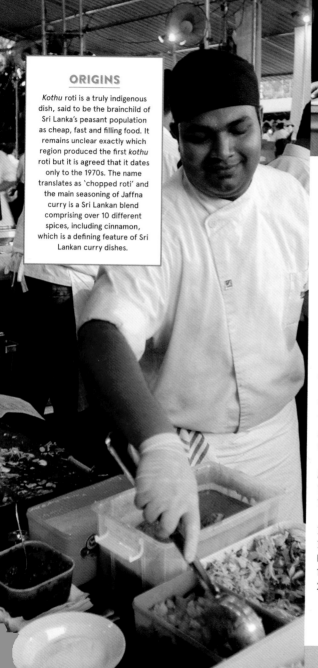

ORIGINS

Kothu roti is a truly indigenous dish, said to be the brainchild of Sri Lanka's peasant population as cheap, fast and filling food. It remains unclear exactly which region produced the first *kothu* roti but it is agreed that it dates only to the 1970s. The name translates as 'chopped roti' and the main seasoning of Jaffna curry is a Sri Lankan blend comprising over 10 different spices, including cinnamon, which is a defining feature of Sri Lankan curry dishes.

YOU'LL NEED

Lamb Curry

1 tbs vegetable oil
1 medium onion, peeled and chopped
3 cloves of garlic, peeled and crushed
1 green chilli, chopped
500g (1lb) stewing lamb, diced
1 tbs curry powder
½ tsp cumin seeds
1 tbs garam masala
Water

Gothamba Roti

225g (8oz) self-raising flour
1 tsp salt
1 tbs vegetable oil
About ½ cup (125mL) water
Oil for brushing and frying

Kothu Roti

1 tbs vegetable oil
1 medium onion, peeled and chopped
½ tsp mustard seeds
½ tsp cumin seeds
Handful of curry leaves
1 green chilli, chopped
2 eggs, beaten

SRI LANKA

KOTHU ROTI

SERVES 6

The cooking of this fiery jumble of chopped *Gothamba* roti,
a fried flatbread, mixed with a meat or vegetable stew spiced
with Jaffna curry powder makes wonderful streetside viewing.

METHOD

1 Make the curry. Heat the oil in a pan and fry
the onion, garlic and chilli until the onions are
soft but not brown. Add the lamb and brown.
Add the spices and cook for 3 minutes. Cover
with water and simmer until the lamb is tender
(at least an hour).

2 To make the roti dough, combine all the
ingredients (apart from the extra oil) until the
mixture starts to come away from the sides of
the bowl. Turn out the mixture and knead until
soft, adding flour or water to get a smooth,
but not sticky, dough. Rest for half an hour.

3 Divide the dough into six balls, then roll out
each to a thickness of 2–3mm (⅛in). Take one
and brush a little oil on the bottom third and
fold towards the middle. Repeat with the top
third. Turn 90 degrees clockwise and repeat
with the bottom and top thirds. Repeat for

each roti. Heat the oil in a pan and flatten
each roti with a rolling pin. Fry each on one
side until the top puffs up and the bottom is
blistered. Turn over and repeat. Cook the rest
of the rotis.

4 To make the *kothu* roti, heat the oil in
a pan and fry the onion, mustard seeds,
cumin seeds, curry leaves and chilli for a few
minutes. Set the mixture to one side of the
pan and scramble the eggs in the other half.

5 Slice the rotis into strips, add to the pan
with the lamb curry and stir-fry to blend and
heat. Serve immediately.

TIP *The roti and the curry can be prepared
a day in advance and assembled just before
serving. Store-bought roti is an acceptable
substitute if time is tight. Ensure the curry has
plenty of gravy to be soaked up by roti.*

TASTING NOTES

Street entertainment doesn't get better than watching the street vendors at work making
kothu roti. Think saliva-inducing aromas of curry and roti sizzling on a smoking-hot griddle
combined with a melodic cacophony of clanking oversized metal dough-scrapers that shred
and mix the roti with a spicy meat gravy. What might sound like stodgy fare – bread, curry,
egg and vegetables seasoned with chillies and the rich local Jaffna curry powder – is in fact
a feast for the senses: golden-yellow, aromatic, and an addictive melange of explosively hot
and savoury flavours. Despite its humble beginnings, the dish is now considered a Sri Lankan
staple, including as a midnight 'snack' for clubbing types. ● *by Johanna Ashby*

ORIGINS

Byzantine Greeks sprinkled their flatbreads with olive oil and herbs. Known as *pita*, these were the precursors of the pizza. It is not known if the Turkish nomads who conquered Byzantine territory adopted the idea, or if Turkish pizzas are an adaptation of the Italian dish. Adding to the culinary conundrum, the word *lahmacun* comes from the Arabic *lahm biajin*, 'meat and dough'.

YOU'LL NEED

Crust
4 cups (600g) plain flour
1¼ cups (300mL) water
¼ cup (60mL) olive oil
3 tsp instant yeast
Salt (sprinkle)

Topping
2 large, ripe tomatoes
1 large, ripe red capsicum
1 large onion, peeled and chopped
1 bunch of parsley
250g (9oz) ground lamb or beef
1 tbs tomato salsa or sugo
¼ cup (60mL) olive oil
Red paprika powder
Ground cumin
Ground black pepper
Salt to taste
Red chilli flakes to serve
Lemon segments to serve

TASTING NOTES

With a thin, light crust, *lahmacun* are pulled from the oven, sprinkled with chilli flakes (often a distinctive, dark variety known as *isot*, from the city of Urfa in Turkey's southeast), and served rolled up in a paper bag. Your first bite will be mostly thin crust, crisp and flaky, with a hint of the delights within to fire your appetite. As you reach the moist, aromatic meat mixture, you'll notice a hint of tomato-salsa sweetness, offset by smouldering chilli and tart lemon juice. The sweet-meaty-spicy combo will tempt you back for more. There's no shame in that: most punters buy a stack and proceed through them, liberally strewing each successive one with more chilli as their palates blaze. ● *by Will Gourlay*

TURKEY

LAHMACUN

A petite, rolled-up, crunchy pizza crust bursting with the sweet tang of minced lamb and the zest of fiery chilli flakes, *lahmacun* is Turkey's oh-so-addictive street snack.

METHOD

1 Combine all the crust ingredients in a bowl to create a dough. Knead thoroughly and leave to rise for at least an hour.

2 Tear off balls of dough, about enough to fill your palm. On a board dusted with flour, roll out the dough thinly with a rolling pin to form the *lahmacun* bases. Ideally each one should be about 20cm (8in) in diameter and 2–3mm (⅛in) thick.

3 For the topping, place the tomatoes, red capsicum, onion and parsley in a food processor and blend until the mixture has the consistency of a thin sauce.

4 Place in a mixing bowl with the ground meat, salsa or sugo, olive oil, paprika, cumin, pepper and salt. Manually mix until all the ingredients are integrated. The mix should be slightly moist.

5 Ladle a portion of the topping on to each base, spreading evenly.

6 Place the discs into a pizza oven or standard kitchen oven (preheated to around 220°C/430°F) for 5–8 minutes (until base is just crisp and topping is sizzling).

7 Sprinkle the *lahmacun* with chilli flakes and/or a squeeze of lemon juice as desired.

YOU'LL NEED

1 tbs peanut/olive oil
500g (1lb) minced chicken
3–4 dried red chillies
2 kaffir lime leaves, sliced
½ red onion, peeled and
  thinly sliced
2 spring onions (scallions),
  finely chopped
¼ cup (60mL) chicken stock
1 tbs cornflour
2–3 tbs fish sauce (to taste)
1 tsp sugar
Juice of 1 lime
4 tbs uncooked sticky rice or
  3–4 tbs chopped cashews
Cos lettuce
¼ cup fresh mint leaves,
  chopped
Handful of fresh basil, ripped
  into pieces

ORIGINS

Arguments rage as to *larb*'s
roots. Some say it originated
in Laos, others that it has the
same roots as steak tartare
– simply raw meat and onions
– and was spread with Haw
merchants from the southwest
of China into northern Thailand.
Whatever, it's known as a dish
of northeast Thailand and Laos,
although regional variations
abound – from pounded raw
buffalo meat and offal to cooked
chicken and pork, though the
dressing is always spicy and rich.

SERVES 4

LAOS/NORTHERN THAILAND

LARB

Minced meat, shards of crisp red shallot, lime juice, herbs, roasted rice powder and dried chillies... *larb* can be fresh and fragrant, skipping across the tongue, or seriously, pungently powerful.

LARB GAI

METHOD

1 Heat the oil in a large wok over high heat.

2 Add the minced chicken and stir for 2 minutes, until brown.

3 Add the dried chillies, kaffir lime leaves, sliced onion and spring onions and fry for 2 minutes.

4 In a jug, mix together the stock, cornflour, fish sauce, sugar and lime juice, then pour into the chicken mixture.

5 Reduce the heat to medium-high and cook for 3–4 minutes.

6 If using the sticky rice, put it in a dry-frying pan and stir over medium-high heat for 6–8 minutes. When the rice makes a 'popping' sound, transfer it to a pestle and mortar and grind it to a coarse powder.

7 Transfer the warm chicken to a big serving bowl, pour over the ground rice/chopped cashews and accompany with lettuce, fresh mint, fresh basil and – if you can take it – extra chilli!

TIP *Chicken is the classic choice for this Thai dish, but pork/beef or even firm tofu would certainly suffice.*

TASTING NOTES

This is a dish that can be ethereally delicate (albeit with a proper chilli punch), or viscerally carnivorous (buffalo hide, spleen, heart and liver can be a little testing when raw). As ever, balance is everything. The meat (cooked or uncooked) is finely minced or ground, and cooked (or bathed) in a dressing made of meat broth with dried red chilli powder. Optional lime juice adds citrus zing. In the Laotian version, shallots and garlic are blackened over an open flame first, to give that distinctive charred tang. Various herbs play their usual fragrant role, and the addition of roasted, ground glutinous rice powder at the end not only adds crunch, but a nutty depth too. ● *by Tom Parker Bowles*

ORIGINS

Laos claims *larb moo* as its national dish. That hasn't stopped its neighbours in northeastern Thailand from taking it, transforming it and laying claim to their own version of *larb*. The Lao variety tends to omit any limes and fish sauce, opting instead for dried spices and chillies. For a truly authentic taste, *larb* is sometimes made using raw pork. Because of a significant Lao population in the USA, it's relatively easy to find there.

SERVES 2

NORTHEASTERN THAILAND & LAOS

LARB MOO

A simple salad packed with fiery, fresh flavours, *larb moo* wows you with superb minced pork and its combination of zinging herbs and chillies give it a killer kick.

YOU'LL NEED

1 cup (250mL) water
350g (12oz) minced pork
3 tbs chopped spring onions (scallions)
2 tbs chopped fresh coriander (cilantro) leaves
2 tbs chopped mint leaves
3 tbs lime juice
2 tbs fish sauce
1 tbs sugar
1 tbs ground roasted rice
1 tbs chilli powder
Cucumber and sticky or steamed rice to serve

METHOD

1 Boil the water then add the pork and cook for 2 minutes.

2 Once cooked, drain the pork in a strainer.

3 Place the pork in a mixing bowl and combine with the spring onions, coriander leaves and most of the mint.

4 Keep mixing and season with the lime juice, fish sauce, sugar, ground roasted rice and chilli powder.

5 Garnish with leftover mint.

6 Serve with cucumber and sticky (or steamed) rice.

TASTING NOTES

Eating this is an experience. You can opt for the fork-and-spoon method favoured by most Thais, but you can also be creative. Grab a lettuce leaf and pile a spoonful of *larb moo* on to it. Wrap the leaf into a small ball, pop it in your mouth and wait a second. The fusion of crunchy lettuce, spicy pork and fresh herbs all simultaneously competing for your attention is unforgettable. It will be accompanied by sticky rice contained in a small bamboo holder. Work the rice into a ball with your right hand, dip it into the *larb* and you'll be eating it just like the locals. If your *larb* is too spicy, munch on the side of cucumber. ● *by Mark Beales*

ORIGINS

Mangue verte may have evolved from *buggai*, a spicy green mango chutney. It's served with *thieboudjenne*, the national lunch, and the communal bowl in which it's served is cordially fought over. It may also have travelled up from Guinea-Bissau or Senegal's Casamance region, famous for having the best mangoes. There, green-mango juice is made by sun-drying the unripe fruit for three days, then boiling it and adding sugar.

SERVES 1

SENEGAL

MANGUE VERTE

Mangue verte (green mango) has more in common with potato chips than yellow mangoes. On a hot day, it proves a refreshing combination of salty, crunchy and tart.

YOU'LL NEED

1 green mango
½ small lime (optional)
salt or a crushed Jumbo (a kind of MSG stock cube) or other stock cube
chilli powder

METHOD

1 Peel the mango, then slice it.

2 Squirt a bit of lime juice on to the fruit if you like it tangy, and toss.

3 Sprinkle over the crushed stock cube, salt and chilli to taste.

TASTING NOTES

Green-mango season coincides with Senegal's hottest period of year, so it is a time of bittersweet anticipation. It's sunny, the air is dry, and everyone is walking more slowly. Even the women who sell *mangues vertes*, their hair tied up in colourful scarves, prepare the snack at a sedate pace, slicing the mango of your choosing into a bag and shaking it up with the toppings. The mango is hard as an apple, and the first taste is salty and crunchy, followed by the bite of the chilli, but then the mango comes through, its sweetness just a glimmer and its sourness a fruity kick – a burst of energy on a hot day.

● *by Amy Karafin, with Maïmouna Ciss*

ORIGINS

Many years ago, in the town of Ciqikou in Chongqing, a woman invented a stew to help her father-in-law, a butcher, make the best of the offal from the day's slaughter. She boiled up a cauldron of broth using a pig's head and bones and some peas, then added offal, spices and, on a whim, blood curd. The last, she discovered, became tender and tofu-like with prolonged cooking. The resulting stew was so delicious, it became a hit.

YOU'LL NEED

3 tbs oil
1½ tbs Sichuan peppercorns
2 tbs crushed dried chillies
20 cumin seeds
1 Chinese star anise
8 tbs peeled and grated garlic
50g (2oz) Sichuan broad-
   bean-chilli paste
3 cups (750mL) pork or
   chicken stock, plus extra if
   needed
4 slices of fresh ginger
150g (5oz) leek, cut into 3cm
   (1¼in) pieces
200g (7oz) honeycomb beef
   tripe, cut into 1½cm (½in)
   slices
250g (9oz) blood curd, cut
   into 1cm (⅓in) slices
1 yellow eel or any white fish,
   meat only, cut into 1½cm
   (½in) slices
300g (11oz) bean sprouts
2 handfuls of soaked black
   fungus
1 tbs Chinese yellow wine
1 tbs light soy sauce
2 tsp Chinese black vinegar
Salt to taste
Handful of fresh coriander
   (cilantro) leaves, roughly
   chopped

SERVES 3

SICHUAN, CHINA

MAO XUE WANG

Literally 'fur blood extravaganza', this is a dish for demons – blood curd, entrails, eel and other delectable fare swirl in a simmering broth laced with chillies and Sichuan peppercorns.

METHOD

1 Heat the oil to a pan, then add the Sichuan peppercorns, crushed dried chillies, cumin seeds and Chinese star anise and fry for a few seconds until fragrant.

2 Add the grated garlic and Sichuan broad-bean-chilli paste and saute for another few seconds.

3 Pour the stock into the pan. Throw in the ginger, leek, tripe and blood curd. Bring to a boil then let it simmer on a low heat for 45 minutes. Check the level of the stock every 15 minutes and make sure none of the ingredients are sticking to the bottom of the pan. Add more stock if necessary.

4 Add the eel, bean sprouts, black fungus, wine, soy sauce and vinegar and let simmer for another 10 minutes.

5 Taste and add salt if necessary.

6 Sprinkle on the coriander and serve.

TASTING NOTES

Mao xue wang is one of the hottest dishes in China's hottest cuisine. First up, you'll surprise your palate by the fast heat and fruitiness of the dried red peppers and the slow tongue-numbing quality (*ma-la* in Putonghua) of the Sichuan peppercorns, which lends depth to the heat. Venture further and a feast of textures awaits – silky (blood curd), chewy (heart), gelatinous (sea cucumber), firm (eel), crunchy (black fungus, bean sprouts), rubbery (cuttlefish), stringy (tripe), spongy (cooked tofu)... You'll find the mild flavours of the ingredients offer some respite from the heat, cooling your lips and tongue just enough that they can wrap themselves around the next titillating piece. ● *by Piera Chen*

YOU'LL NEED

2 tsp plus 1 tbs *huajiao* (Sichuan pepper)
1 tsp cornflour
2 tsp water
2 tbs Shaoxing wine
1 tbs soy sauce
¼ cup (60mL) chicken stock
680g (1½lb) medium-firm bean curd, cut in 2.5cm (1in) cubes
¼ cup (60mL) vegetable oil
110g (¼lb) beef, thinly sliced
3 cloves of garlic, peeled and diced
Small knob of fresh ginger, peeled and diced
2 tbs fermented broad-bean-chilli sauce
¼ cup (60mL) chilli-sesame oil
3 *suanmiao* (wild leek shoots), or you can substitute spring onions, tender parts only, bias sliced

ORIGINS

Mapo doufu means 'pockmarked old lady's bean curd', (*ma* means pockmarked, *po* means elder lady). In late 19th-century Chengdu, Chen Mapo ran an eatery on a route travelled by porters who worked up a hunger carrying heavy goods. As one story goes, a labourer moving rapeseed oil asked Chen Mapo to cook lunch in exchange for some of his haul. She tossed together what she had, topped it with infused chilli oil, and her namesake dish was born.

BJ/BLUE JEAN IMAGES © GETTY IMAGES, LMR GROUP © ALAMY

SICHUAN, CHINA

MAPO DOUFU

SERVES 2

Silky bean curd, beef and leek sprouts swimming in a chilli-black-bean sauce that glows a fiery red sums up Sichuan cuisine in one bowl – feisty, comforting and tongue-numbingly good.

METHOD

1 Toast 2 tsp of *huajiao* in a wok over a medium-high heat, stirring continuously, for 30 seconds. Transfer to a mortar and pestle. Let it cool, then grind finely.

2 Whisk together the cornflour and water, then add the wine, soy sauce and stock.

3 Cover the bean curd in water in a saucepan, bring to the boil and boil for about 5 minutes. Drain.

4 Pour the oil into the wok set over a medium heat. Add the remaining 1 tbs *huajiao*. Cook for 30 seconds, stirring continuously until you see a thin wisp of smoke. Remove the peppercorns, retaining the oil.

5 Turn the heat to medium-high. Add the

beef. Stir-fry for about 30 seconds.

6 Add the garlic and ginger. Stir-fry for 30 seconds.

7 Add the broad-bean-chilli sauce. Stir-fry for 30 seconds.

8 Pour in the cornflour mixture. Bring to a boil, stirring constantly.

9 Carefully add the bean curd and chilli oil, trying not to break up the bean curd. Bring to the boil and then immediately turn off the heat. Transfer to a serving bowl.

10 Top with a dusting of the ground *huajiao* and *suanmiao*.

TASTING NOTES

Known for its distinctive *ma-la* (numbing and hot) flavour, Sichuan cuisine (called Chuan) is distinguished by spicy, oil-based sauces, *huajiao* (Sichuan pepper) and dried chillies. In a dish of *mapo doufu*, that combination is utterly transfixing – it quickens the pulse, dilates the pupils, and drops you into a euphoric stupor. In proper *mapo doufu*, tender bean curd luxuriates with slivers of beef in a generous pool of dayglo-red sauce – a salty, spicy, numbing stew of sorts that's over-the-top good. Whether in an open-air street stall or a fancy restaurant, it is best accompanied with a plate of simple, stir-fried greens – and maybe some rice to temper the heat. ● *by Tienlon Ho*

YOU'LL NEED

Tamarind paste stuffing

6 tbs tamarind pulp
1 tsp palm sugar
¼ tsp ground cumin
½ tsp salt

Pakoda

10–15 large green chillies, with
    stems
60g (2oz) gram (chickpea)
    flour
1½ tbs rice flour
¼ tsp baking powder
¼ tsp salt
½ tsp ground chilli
½ tsp ground turmeric
½ tsp whole cumin seeds
A little cold water
Vegetable oil for deep-frying
Lime chutney, chopped
    onions and fresh coriander
    (cilantro) leaves to serve

ORIGINS

The translation of *pakoda* is
mundane – it means 'cooked
lumps' – but the dish is as
ancient as the Indian hills. Many
trace the origins of the *pakoda*
to Uttar Pradesh, famed for
its fusion of Hindu and Muslim
cooking ideas, but the word
is Sanskrit, placing the *pakoda*
on a far older calendar. The
Sanskrit language was spoken
as early as 2000 BC, so this
could well be one of the world's
first fritters.

SERVES 4
AS A SNACK

INDIA & PAKISTAN

MIRCHI KA PAKODA

**Forget chilli poppers or Padrón peppers – India's *mirchi ka pakoda*
(whole green chillies dipped in lentil-flour batter and deep-fried)
take spiciness to a whole new, literally mouthwatering, level.**

METHOD

1 Mix together the tamarind paste stuffing
ingredients to form a thick paste.

2 Using a small knife, make a cut in the side
of each chilli and press in a teaspoon of the
tamarind paste stuffing.

3 Combine the gram flour, rice flour, baking
powder, salt, ground chilli, ground turmeric
and cumin seeds and mix into a thick batter
with a little cold water.

4 Heat the oil in a large pan suitable for deep-
frying until the surface shimmers.

5 Holding it by its stem, dip each chilli into
the batter until it is thickly coated, then pour
a teaspoon of batter over the chilli and drop
quickly and carefully into the hot oil.

6 Deep-fry the chilli *pakoda* in small batches
for 2–3 minutes until golden brown, then
remove from the oil and drain.

7 Serve with lime chutney, chopped onions
and coriander leaves.

TASTING NOTES

For newbies in India, *pakoda* seem like a safe bet. Battered vegetables. Sounds risk-free.
Even your first few bites of these friendly-looking brown parcels will probably be reassuringly
mild. And it's at this point, after you have been lulled into a false sense of security by
chickpeas, onion, spinach, potato and eggplant, that *mirchi ka pakoda* chooses to strike: this
scorching snack conceals a whole green chilli, seeds and all. Fast cooking in hot oil preserves
the heat, so what goes into your mouth is as explosive as what went into the batter. Seek out
regional variations: in Gujarat, the *mirchi ka pakoda* are stuffed with tamarind and mango
powder; in Rajasthan, the chillies are laced with spiced potatoes. ● *by Joe Bindloss*

ORIGINS

Mustard as a condiment harks back to Roman times, when seeds were ground and blended with young wine ('must') for a fiery flavour, hence the Latin *mustum ardens* – 'burning must' – that's reputedly the origin of the English word mustard. The tongue-tickler has been made in the Netherlands since at least 1457 in Doesburg, and is put to excellent use in this rich, thick, creamy broth – central heating in a bowl.

THE NETHERLANDS

MOSTERDSOEP

SERVES 4

It's a condiment, it's a soup, it's a taste sensation: finest whole-grain Dutch mustard soup warms the cockles (and tongue) like only a steaming serving of spice-spiked chowder can.

YOU'LL NEED

1 medium-sized onion, peeled and finely chopped
50g (2oz) butter
50g (2oz) sifted flour
4 cups (1L) stock (chicken or vegetable)
1 tbs grainy mustard (ideally from Groningen)
1 tbs smooth mustard
½ tsp mustard seeds
Scant ½ cup (100mL) cream (or crème fraîche)
Salt and pepper to taste

Garnish
Freshly chopped chives
150g (5oz) bacon, fried in crispy bits
Crusty rolls or bread to serve

METHOD

1 In a saucepan, slowly fry the onion in the butter until softened and translucent.

2 Stir in the flour to form a paste.

3 Gradually add the stock, stirring constantly to prevent lumps forming and to create a smooth liquid.

4 Add the mustards and mustard seeds.

5 Simmer on a low heat for a few minutes, adding the cream just before serving.

6 Season to taste.

7 Ladle into bowls, scatter over the chopped chives and bacon bits and serve with crusty rolls or bread.

TIP *For extra richness, cream cheese (smeerkaas) can be added to the mixture before the final heating. Finely chopped chillies add extra potency – if you feel it's needed!*

TASTING NOTES

The wind blows chill along the canal as sunlight glints off the ice. Shivering, you spot a cafe and duck inside; the cosy atmosphere envelops you in a warm hug of gezelligheid. There's one thing on your mind, and you want it in your belly: mosterdsoep. You've just time for a sip of jenever (Dutch gin) before a steaming bowl appears, chives floating on its golden surface. Liberally sprinkling spekjes (crispy bacon bits), you gingerly sip a spoonful, savouring the smooth richness. A tickle teases your nostrils as the heat of the mustard sneaks up on you. It's a strange sensation, and weirdly addictive – you can't tell if it hurts or excites. Best try another mouthful to be sure... ● *by Paul Bloomfield*

ORIGINS

Ignacio Anaya, called 'Nacho' by his friends, was the maître d' of a restaurant in the Mexican border town of Piedras Negras, which was popular with the wives of American military officers stationed in nearby Eagle Pass, Texas, during World War II. One day, when the cook was away, quick-thinking Nacho served the ladies a plate of tortilla chips covered in melted cheese with pickled jalapeños. He called it 'Nacho's special', and the beloved snack was born.

SERVES 4
AS A SNACK

NORTHERN MEXICO & SOUTHWESTERN USA

NACHOS

Is there a more perfect bar food than nachos? An addictive combination of crispy tortilla chips smothered in melted cheese, salsa and a range of toppings, they're perfect for sharing.

YOU'LL NEED

500g (1lb) tortilla chips
230g (8oz) Cheddar cheese, grated
100g (3½oz) pickled jalapeños
Sour cream, salsa and Mexican hot sauce to serve

METHOD

1 Cover a baking tray with tortilla chips and sprinkle liberally with the grated cheese.

2 Top with pickled jalapeños.

3 Bake at 175°C (350°F) for 10–15 minutes or until the cheese is melted.

4 Serve with sour cream, salsa and Mexican hot sauce (such as Valentina).

TASTING NOTES

Though invented in Mexico, it's the USA that is up to its ears in nachos – every mid-range chain in the country has its own 'fully-loaded' version creaking under the weight of beef mince and sour cream, and every ballpark serves buckets of tortilla chips drowned in a hot, creamy, slightly spicy neon-orange cheese product called 'nacho cheese'. These are definitely good, but for our money, the best kind of nacho is the pared-down dish found at classier Tex-Mex joints: fresh hot tortilla chips smothered with real Cheddar cheese, a thin layer of refried beans, a handful of pickled jalapeños and a healthy dollop of guacamole and house-made *pico de gallo* salsa. ● *by Emily Matchar*

ORIGINS

The *bungkus* form of this dish – a small portable pyramid wrapped in a banana leaf – probably developed as the ideal take-anywhere breakfast for rural folk working from dawn in the fields. A more creative origin story, however, comes from Melaka in Malaysia. This tells of a girl who accidentally spilled coconut milk into cooking rice. When her mother asked about the different flavour the girl said 'nasi le, mak' – it's just rice, mother – and the phrase stuck!

YOU'LL NEED

Coconut rice
2 cups rice, rinsed
A knot of pandan leaves, if available
1 cup (250mL) coconut milk
1 cup (250mL) water
Salt

Tamarind water
1 cup (250mL) water
2 tsp tamarind pulp

Anchovy sambal
1 cup dried anchovies (*ikan bilis*), if available
1 tsp shrimp paste (*belacan*)
4 shallots or 2 small onions, peeled
1 clove of garlic, peeled
5–10 dried chillies, seeded
Peanut oil or similar
½ red onion, peeled and thinly sliced
1 tbs sugar
Salt to taste

To serve
Quartered hard-boiled eggs
Crisp fried fish
Fried salted peanuts
Cucumber slices

SERVES 4

MALAYSIA & SINGAPORE

NASI LEMAK

The fragrance of this breakfast-until-brunch dish of steamed coconut rice topped with sambal (chilli sauce), egg, cucumber, peanuts and fish wafts daily from waking households across the Malay Peninsula.

METHOD

1 First make the coconut rice. Cook the ingredients together in a rice cooker or bring to the boil in a pan, cover and simmer for 12 minutes or so. Turn off and leave covered for 15 minutes.

2 To make the tamarind water, put the water and tamarind in a bowl. Squeeze the tamarind from time to time. Strain after 15 minutes and discard pulp.

3 For the anchovy sambal, rinse and drain the anchovies. Heat a frying pan over a medium heat, add the anchovies and fry until light brown. Set aside.

4 Grind the shrimp paste, shallots or onions, garlic and seeded chillies in a pestle and mortar, or whizz in a food processor.

5 Heat the peanut oil and fry the spice paste. While stirring, add the red onion slices, anchovies, tamarind water, sugar and salt.

6 Simmer for around 15 minutes, until the sauce thickens.

7 Serve *nasi lemak* with sambal on the side. Garnish with quartered hard-boiled eggs, crisp fried fish, fried salted peanuts and cucumber slices.

TASTING NOTES

Unwrapping a green pyramid of *nasi lemak* is a ritual to savour, with its contrasts of smooth rice, piquant sambal and the crunch of raw cucumber and crispy fish. Part of the pleasure is discovering what's inside. Each cook has their own version of sambal (*pedas* is seriously spicy; *manis* is made spicy-sweet with the distinctive addition of palm sugar) and combination of garnish (omelette instead of hard-boiled egg; fried chicken wing instead of fish). It's the perfect picnic food: fresh, readily available and served in biodegradable packaging. Traditionally *nasi lemak* is eaten with the fingers, but most *bungkus* come with plastic spoons. Or sit and eat from a plate at a food market watching the stallholders at work. ● *by Virginia Jealous*

YOU'LL NEED

1 tbs olive oil
1 small onion, peeled and
  chopped
'Nduja to taste
400g (14oz) good-quality
  tinned Italian tomatoes
480g (1lb) dried pasta
Grated *ricotta salata* (salted
  ricotta)

ORIGINS

Created as a way to use up
a pig's more humble parts,
'nduja has become a Calabrian
speciality. The Spanish imported
chilli peppers to Italy in the 16th
century, but it's possible *'nduja*
('an-DO-yah') developed from
the French 'andouille', a coarse,
spicy smoked-pork and garlic
sausage, as the pronunciation
is similar. But this incarnation –
with its extraordinary marriage
between taste and heat – was
born in Spilinga, in Calabria's
deep south.

SERVES 4

CALABRIA, ITALY

'NDUJA

In Calabria, the sunbaked toe of the Italian boot, pigs roam almost wild, grazing on chestnuts, marjoram and spearmint. *'Nduja*, a spreadable salami, is formed from the alchemy of their fragrant meat and fiercely hot Calabrese peppers.

PASTA POMMODORO E 'NDUJA

METHOD

1 Heat the oil in a saucepan and gently cook the onions until caramelised. While they are cooking, put on a pot of salted water to boil for the pasta.

2 When the onions have softened and have a golden colour, add the *'nduja* to them and let the salami paste melt over the gentle heat. The more you add, the punchier the sauce, so use as much as you feel it needs.

3 Once all the salami fat has melted, mix in the tomatoes, and continue cooking the sauce as you cook the pasta, which you'll now add to the boiling water.

4 Cook the pasta until al dente (still has some bite), drain and mix in the sauce.

5 Serve topped with a sprinkling of *ricotta salata*.

TASTING NOTES

The salami paste is deep, dark, chilli red. Try it spread on a chunk of locally made bread. A bite starts with the blowtorch blast of the infamous Calabrese peppers, which then slowly subsides, allowing the powerful, creamy flavour of the pork to foreground. The complex, punchy taste also enhances multiple Calabrese dishes, such as pasta with *'nduja* and *fagioli* (beans). To outsiders, Calabria has an air of mystery, infamous for its mafia (the 'Ndrangheta) and wild countryside strewn with higgledy-piggledy towns. The best place to try *'nduja* is here, near Spilinga, where it was invented. Warm your cockles with it in autumn or winter at a rustic neighbourhood trattoria, or as part of a picnic overlooking wooded landscapes. ● *by Abigail Blasi*

ORIGINS

The spice may have gone out of Portugal's political relationship with its former colony Guinea-Bissau, but the recipes are still going strong. *Ostras picantes* is the marriage of Portugal's culinary traditions and the sizzle of a small seafaring nation. Oysters are easy to get in Guinea-Bissau and unlike other parts of the world, here they've never lost their working-class roots. The season generally runs from December to July, after which oysters are best avoided due to the heavy rains.

SERVES 6

GUINEA-BISSAU

OSTRAS PICANTES

Nothing brings out Guinea-Bissau's charms more than eating *ostras picantes* – saltwater oysters from mangrove-fringed islands bathed in a loose lime sauce spiked with hot pepper – as the sun sets.

YOU'LL NEED

Oysters
8–15 small- to medium-sized
  oysters per person

Sauce
Handful of diced hot chilli
  peppers
Pinch of salt
¼ of a bouillon cube
10 large, fresh, squeezed
  limes

METHOD

1 Remove the grill pan from barbecue and throw the oysters, in their shells, on to the naked burning coals.

2 For the sauce, in a grinder or mortar, pound the diced chilli peppers together with the salt and bouillon cube until it forms a fine damp powder.

3 Add the juice of the fresh limes and mix well.

4 Remove the oysters from the coals when they crack open, releasing hot steam.

5 Serve the oysters in a large communal bowl, with a small bowl of sauce served separately.

6 Each diner receives a blunt knife and colourful tea towel to prise open the oysters. Dip and enjoy.

TASTING NOTES

Often used as an aperitif ahead of a night out dancing, the oysters are grilled in their shells in a loose pyramid pile that's flung directly on to burning charcoal. They're ready when they pop open, giving off super-heated steam. Diners grab a small colourful cloth and a short blunt knife, prising out the briny beasts and dunking them into the thin spicy sauce – made from fresh local lime, salt, bouillon cube and lots of cut chilli pepper, all bound together using a mortar. The resulting taste combines the crisp flavour of lime with memories of hot summer days on the beach, wrapped up with hints of roasted timber and fire. ● *by Kate Thomas*

ORIGINS

In the Bahasa Indonesia and Malay languages, the word 'otak' means brains. But don't let this keep you from trying *otak-otak*; the name comes from the colour and consistency of the dish, not its ingredients. Originating in Malaysia and Indonesia, *otak-otak* migrated to Singapore, where it quickly became a hawker-centre staple. Food-obsessed Singaporeans are said to cross the causeway into Muar in southern Malaysia for a taste of that town's *otak-otak* (said to be the region's best).

YOU'LL NEED

400g (14oz) deboned mackerel, minced
1 small onion, finely chopped
1 egg, lightly beaten
½ small turmeric leaf, thinly sliced
2 kaffir lime leaves, thinly sliced
2 tbs laksa leaves (Vietnamese mint), thinly sliced
1 tbs oil (optional)
½–¾ cup coconut cream
1 tbs sugar
salt, to taste
banana leaves, cut to 20cm x 10cm (8in x 4in) and microwaved for 1 min to soften

For the spice paste

1.25cm (½in) turmeric root (or ¼ tsp powdered turmeric)
2–4 red chillies
4 pieces galangal, sliced (ginger can be substituted)
1 lemongrass stalk
3 candlenuts
2 garlic cloves
6 shallots
1 tsp *belacan* (shrimp paste), dry-roasted

MAKES 8

SINGAPORE, MALAYSIA AND INDONESIA

OTAK-OTAK

A hand-held fish, egg and onion pâté that comes in its own natural (and biodegradable) package? For convenience, deliciousness and environmental friendliness, this spicy Southeast Asian treat takes first prize.

METHOD

1 Grind the spice paste ingredients to a fine paste.

2 Combine the spice paste with all the other ingredients (except the banana leaves) in a mixing bowl. Adjust to taste with salt and sugar.

3 Spoon 2 tbs of the mixture on to each banana leaf. Fold the leaf and secure it with a toothpick on both ends.

4 Grill or barbecue for about 10 minutes and serve.

TASTING NOTES

At first glance, the sight of long green leaves charring may lead the uninitiated into thinking that *otak-otak* is some sort of grilled tropical vegetable. But the charred green leaf is the packaging only – inside you'll find a gelatinous cake that's spicy and aromatic (with just a hint of the ocean). *Otak-otak* is best eaten at a streetside stall or inside a hawker centre, perhaps with a bottle of Tiger beer or an iced Milo. Though generally eaten as a side dish with other items (skewered chicken or grilled prawns make for a great combination), four or five *otak-otaks* should be enough to hold you over until your next meal.

This recipe comes to us from Ruqxana Vasanwala at Cookery Magic in Singapore (cookerymagic.com). ● *by Joshua Samuel Brown*

YOU'LL NEED

4 handfuls of palm nuts
Handful of hot chilli peppers
1 clove of garlic, peeled
1 onion, peeled
1 lemon
3 cups (750mL) water
1 large cleaned fish or half a
   chicken
Vegetables (optional)
600g (1lb 5oz) rice

ORIGINS

Made almost exclusively from
local ingredients, palm butter
has been filling bellies in Liberia
for centuries. Some claim it
was a speciality of the Kru
ethnic group from the balmy
southeastern corner of the
country. Today the thick, golden
sauce makes it to daily specials
boards nationwide – from
upscale restaurants to the
simplest of rural 'chop bars'.

SERVES 4

LIBERIA

PALM BUTTER

Rich, buttery and infused with everything from hot pepper and nutty oil to tropical sunshine and sweat, palm butter tastes as if it has all of Liberia locked inside it.

METHOD

1 Add palm nuts to a saucepan filled with boiling water and boil for about 15 minutes until the nuts are semi-soft.

2 In a blender (or with a mortar and pestle) pound the chilli peppers, garlic and onion.

3 Parboil the chopped fish or chicken with the blended pepper, garlic and onion mixture in water. Vegetables such as mushrooms, zucchini, tomatoes or aubergines (eggplants) can also be added.

4 Next pound the softened palm nuts in a blender (or with a mortar and pestle) until they form a pulp.

5 Add water and press the pulp through a strainer into a saucepan. Discard the fibres and kernels that are left in the strainer. The remaining pulp should contain the oil and fruit of the palm nuts, as well as the water.

6 Heat the pulp, adding extra water if necessary. Add the fish or chicken to the heated palm butter and boil until the mixture is the consistency of Indian curry sauce.

7 Cook the rice and serve the palm butter over it.

TASTING NOTES

Liberian comfort food at its best, palm butter's rich, fiery taste easily rivals that of the Indian curry. Local joints tend to up the fire factor; useful if you need to sweat out a fever but beware – it can be served hot enough to hurt. In Liberian homes, preparation often takes hours, beginning with boiling, then grinding the palm nuts to extract the oil and jungle flavour. Then blindingly hot spice (known as '*pepe check*') is chucked in, along with salt, garlic, onions, water and palm oil. The resulting sauce, complete with chicken or fish, is poured over rice or thinned with water to make a soup that's typically served with *fufu* (a West African staple made from cassava). ● *by Kate Thomas*

YOU'LL NEED

6 potatoes
Lettuce
2–3 *ají amarillo* peppers
2 tbs vegetable oil
225g (½lb) queso fresco, or
  farmer's cheese, crumbled
  (a reduced-salt feta, mild
  goat's cheese or *ricotta
  salata* can be substituted)
2–3 cups (500–750mL)
  evaporated milk
4 saltine crackers
Salt and pepper to taste
3 eggs, hard-boiled
¼ cup (a handful) of whole
  black Spanish olives

ORIGINS

Some say *papas a la Huancaína* was invented in Chosica, a suburb of Lima, but folklore claims it was invented by a woman from Huancayo, a city in the Mantaro valley and the final stop for a train route from Lima. While the railroad was being built in the late 19th century, women competed with each other to sell workers food – usually potatoes. One market-savvy *señora* doctored hers with a unique sauce and it went on to become a hit.

SERVES 4 AS A STARTER

PERU

PAPAS A LA HUANCAÍNA

This classic Peruvian version of cheese-topped tubers delivers you to the heart of the Andes with a soulful marriage of two indigenous ingredients: potatoes and the *ají amarillo* pepper.

METHOD

1 Scrub, boil and peel potatoes. Allow them to cool and cut in thick slices lengthwise. Arrange on serving plate(s) on top of a few lettuce leaves.

2 Wash and cut the peppers, stripping out the ribs and most of the seeds. Cut into large pieces and saute gently in 1 tsp oil for a few minutes until they begin to soften.

3 Put the peppers, cheese, evaporated milk, remaining oil and saltine crackers into a blender and process until you have a fairly thick sauce. Add extra evaporated milk if the mixture is too thick or saltines if it's too runny. Season with a dash of salt and pepper.

4 Pour the sauce over the potatoes. Cut the eggs in half and arrange on the plate, along with a few olives.

TASTING NOTES

Sauntering around Huancayo's Feria Dominical Sunday market high in the Andes, taking in the array of colourful handicrafts, you're feeling peckish, and stop for a plate of *papas*. That first forkful of cheese-topped potato soothes your palate as the velvety sauce envelops the potato and dissolves on your tongue – there's no hard work involved here. Give yourself a moment to detect the unique fruit and grassiness of the Peruvian *ají* pepper, which shines through before it kicks your tongue on the way down. Add a bit of olive, egg and lettuce for your second bite and you'll get a well-choreographed dance of sweet, salty, smooth and crunchy. Take a sip of *chicha de jora* (corn beer) and repeat. ● *by Caroline Veldhuis*

ORIGINS

Italians have been cooking pasta for nearly a millennium. It is likely that it was brought to Sicily by Arab traders (not, as popular legend has it, imported by Marco Polo from China!), and since then an unknown number of pasta recipes have been developed. *Pasta all'arrabbiata* is one that is especially associated with the lusty, earthy cuisine of Rome, though you can find it on menus and in domestic *cucinas* nationwide.

SERVES 4

ITALY

PASTA ALL'ARRABBIATA

**Literally translating as 'angry pasta', *pasta all'arrabbiata*
is all hot and bothered because of its bright-red sauce,
a spicy mix of tomatoes, garlic and hot chilli flakes.**

YOU'LL NEED

1 medium onion, peeled and
chopped
2 cloves of garlic, peeled and
minced
¼ cup (60mL) olive oil
400g (14oz) tinned tomatoes,
drained
½ tsp red chilli flakes
500g (1lb) dry pasta (penne or
spaghetti)
Salt to taste
100g (3½oz) pecorino cheese,
grated

METHOD

1 Over medium heat, saute the onion and garlic in half of
the oil until golden.

2 Add the tomatoes and chilli and bring to a simmer.

3 Meanwhile, cook the pasta until it is al dente, then drain.

4 Stir the remaining oil into the tomato mixture, season with
salt to taste and pour over the pasta.

5 Serve with freshly grated cheese.

TASTING NOTES

Look for *pasta all'arrabbiata* in Rome's neighbourhood *trattoria*, where rustic dishes are
accompanied by a carafe or two of house Chianti. The beauty of the dish is in its simplicity:
al-dente pasta in a light, bright sauce of garlicky tomatoes, studded with tongue-numbing
dried red chilli flakes. A hearty plateful will keep you full for hours. *Pasta all'arrabbiata*
is also a popular home-cooked meal, the kind of thing your *nonna* throws together in 20
minutes on a Monday evening. If you're lucky enough to befriend a few locals, perhaps
you'll also be lucky enough to be invited to supper – they'll supply the pasta, you bring
the vino. ● *by Emily Matchar*

ORIGINS

Pepperpot is an Amerindian dish, invented by Guyanese natives as a way to preserve meat without refrigeration. The *cassareep* acts as a preservative, allowing cooks to leave the pepperpot on the stove for days to add more and reheat. Traditionally, it is made in a special pot (also called a pepper pot) that retains and imparts flavour from one stew to the next. Legend has it that if you double-dip, the whole batch will spoil!

JOHNNY HAGLUND, PHILIP WILKINS © GETTY IMAGES

GUYANA

PEPPERPOT

Guyana's national dish, this highly spiced meat stew gets its dark colour from *cassareep* – syrup derived from cassava root – and its fiery kick from Caribbean chillies.

YOU'LL NEED

1kg (2lb) stewing beef, cubed
1kg (2lb) ox tail, goat or
  mutton, cubed
Water
1 cup (250mL) *cassareep*
  (available in West Indian
  speciality stores or online)
2 red peppers, seeded
2.5cm (1in) piece dried orange
  or lemon peel
2.5cm (1in) piece of cinnamon
  stick
3 cloves
60g (2oz) sugar
Salt to taste
Bread to serve

METHOD

1 Place the meat in a large pot, adding enough water to cover. Bring to the boil, skim, then reduce the heat to medium-low and simmer for 1 hour.

2 Add the other ingredients, simmering until the meat is tender, up to 3 hours.

3 Serve with bread.

TASTING NOTES

In Guyana, pepperpot is best known as a Christmas dish, its rich, spicy scent perfuming the house on Christmas Eve and into Christmas morning. Extended families gather round the pot for servings of the glossy brown stew, the meat so tender it's falling off the bone. Sop up the juices with a slice of soft homemade plait bread, a braided loaf that resembles Jewish challah. The spice of the chilli warms the back of your throat as you gobble spoonful after spoonful, savouring the deep, complex flavour. If you're not lucky enough to be invited to a Guyanese Christmas, a handful of restaurants in the nation's capital of Georgetown serve the labour-intensive dish. ● *by Emily Matchar*

YOU'LL NEED

For the paste

6 or more small fresh Thai
  chillies
4 cloves of garlic, peeled

For the stir-fry

1 tbs vegetable oil
300g (10½oz) minced pork
1 tbs oyster sauce
1 tbs soy sauce
1 tsp sugar
60ml (¼ cup) water or stock
1 large fresh Thai chilli, thinly
  sliced
75g (3oz) holy basil
4 eggs, fried (optional)

ORIGINS

Today, *phat kaphrao* is
thoroughly entrenched, arguably
one of the most common and
beloved dishes in Thailand. It's
most likely a recent invention,
an example of culinary fusion
that blends Chinese cooking
techniques (wok frying) and Thai
ingredients (chilli, holy basil).
Like many other similar dishes,
the two probably first crossed
paths in central Thailand, where
for more than 200 years, the
Thais and the Chinese have been
swapping culture – and cuisine.

SERVES 4

PHAT KAPHRAO MUU

Minced pork wok-fried with holy basil and no small amount of chilli and garlic: the go-to spicy lunch of the on-the-go Thai.

METHOD

1 In a granite mortar and pestle, pound chillies and garlic until you have a rough paste. Set aside.

2 Place a medium wok over a high heat and add oil.

3 When the oil is smoking, add the pork. Stirring only occasionally, allow to brown slightly for about 2 minutes.

4 Add the oyster sauce, soy sauce and sugar, stirring to combine. Taste and adjust seasoning if necessary. If the mixture is dry and/or sticking to pan, loosen with a tablespoon or two of water or stock.

5 Add large fresh Thai chilli and holy basil, stirring briefly to combine until basil has just begun to wilt, for about 30 seconds.

6 Remove from heat. If serving as part of Thai meal, remove to a large serving platter and serve hot, with rice; if serving over rice, divide among four plates of rice and top each with a fried egg.

TIP *Another aspect of* phat kaphrao *that undoubtedly appeals to diners is its adaptability. Although pork is probably the most popular version of the dish, it can also be made with seafood – squid or shrimp – or minced chicken or beef.*

TASTING NOTES

The number of chillies that goes into an average dish of *phat kaphrao* would undoubtedly shock many outside of Thailand. Yet like many Thai dishes, even the spicy ones, the seasoning of *phat kaphrao* varies from person to version. Serving to augment that chilli burn is holy basil, the eponymous kaphrao, an intensely fragrant, almost spicy leafy herb that thrives in Southeast Asia. And throwing fire on fire is the fact that *phat kaphrao* is served with a small bowl of *phrik nam plaa*, thinly-sliced fresh chillies in fish sauce, the Thai equivalent of the salt shaker. Really the only respite in *phat kaphrao muu* is the fact that it's typically served over rice, topped with a fried egg. ● *by Austin Bush*

ORIGINS

Pho has its origins in the cuisines of France and China and was popularised around the end of the 19th century. The Vietnamese took the rice noodles from their northern neighbour and a taste for red meat from the colonialists, and created something new. Some say *pho* (pronounced 'feu') is derived from the French dish *pot au feu*, while others argue that it is Chinese in origin, stemming from a Cantonese word for noodles, *fan*.

YOU'LL NEED

Broth
10cm (4in) piece of ginger
2 yellow onions
cooking oil
2.25kg (5lb) beef marrow or oxtail bones
4.75l (5 quarts) of water
1 cinnamon stick
1 tsp coriander seeds
1 tbs fennel seeds
5 star anise
2 cardamom pods
6 whole garlic cloves
¼ cup fish sauce
2 tbs sugar
1 tbs salt

Noodles & garnishes
225g (½lb) beef steak
450g (1lb) dried flat rice noodles
10 sprigs mint
10 sprigs coriander leaves (cilantro)
10 sprigs Thai basil
12 sawtooth coriander leaves
½ yellow onion, thinly sliced
2 limes, each cut into 6 thin wedges
2–3 chilli peppers, sliced
450g (1lb) beanshoots
hoisin sauce
hot chilli sauce

TASTING NOTES

Dawn is breaking across Vietnam and the hum of scooter engines has yet to reach its mid-morning crescendo. The *pho* sellers have set up stalls, some little more than a battered collection of metal pans, while others include plastic tables and gleaming trolleys. Whatever you choose, it's the broth that matters. This is the heart and soul of *pho* and should be rich and deeply flavoured, hinting at star anise, cardamom and coriander. The noodles should be freshly made, while the chillies are mild, rather than fierce. Beanshoots add a satisfyingly crunchy texture. A dash of fish sauce, a squeeze of lime, and breakfast is ready. Grab a wobbly chair, sit back and slurp. ● *by Tom Parker Bowles*

SERVES 8

VIETNAM

PHO

The breakfast of champions, this fragrant spiced Vietnamese noodle soup topped with slices of beef, brisket, chicken or meatballs and a squeeze of lime is the perfect wake-up call.

METHOD

Broth

1 Halve the ginger and onions lengthwise and place on a baking sheet. Brush with cooking oil and put on the highest rack under a heated grill (broiler). Grill on high until they begin to char. Turn over to char the other side for a total of 10–15 minutes.

2 Boil enough water in a large pot to cover the beef bones and continue to boil on high for five minutes. Drain, rinse the bones and rinse out the pot. Refill the pot with the bones and the 4.75L of cool water. Bring to the boil then lower to a simmer. Remove any scum that rises to the top.

3 Place the cinnamon stick, coriander seeds, fennel seeds, star anise, cardamom pods and garlic cloves in a mesh bag (alternatively, *pho* spice packets are available at speciality Asian food markets) and add to the broth pot along with the charred onion and ginger and the fish sauce, sugar and salt and simmer for 1½ hours.

4 Discard the spice pack and the onion and continue to simmer for another 1½ hours.

5 Strain the broth and return it to the pot. Adjust salt, fish sauce and sugar to taste.

Noodles & garnishes

1 Slice the beef as thinly as possible across the grain.

2 Cook your noodles according to the packet.

3 Bring the broth back to the boil.

4 Arrange all the other garnishes next to your serving bowls.

5 To serve, fill each bowl with noodles and raw meat slices. Ladle the boiling broth into the bowls – this will cook the beef slices.

6 Garnish with the remaining herbs, onion, lime wedges, chillies, beanshoots and sauces, and serve immediately.

ORIGINS

Though *pica pau* translates as woodpecker, no crimson-quiffed Woodies were harmed in the making of this dish. The moniker merely relates to how it's typically eaten, pecked at with toothpicks. The sauce that smothers the strips of meat may date to the 1960s, when returning emigrant Daniel da Silva tried to adapt French food for the Portuguese palate. Whatever its provenance, it is now one of many staple *petiscos* – a Portuguese equivalent to tapas.

PORTUGAL

PICA PAU

SERVES 4

What's that? *Pica pau* means fried WOODPECKER?! Thankfully, this dish of Portuguese meat-magic might have a misleading name, but ordering the slices of gravy-laden pork loin is certainly no mistake.

YOU'LL NEED

500g (1lb) pork loin
Salt and pepper to taste
Olive oil
2 tbs of butter
½ onion, peeled and sliced
4 cloves of garlic, peeled and sliced
Paprika and chillies to taste
2 cups (500mL) beer (or white wine)
Sliced pickles
Bread to serve

METHOD

1 Cut the meat into thin strips; season with salt and pepper.

2 Heat the oil and butter, then add the onion and garlic and saute until soft.

3 Add the paprika, chillies, more salt and pepper and meat and saute for 10 minutes.

4 Add the beer (or wine). Bring to a boil then simmer for 45 minutes.

5 Stir in the pickles.

6 Serve with bread for dipping.

TIP *Not all recipes contain chillies – the spiciness levels are up to you. Be warned: if you use Portuguese piri-piri chillies, these are hot, hot, hot!*

TASTING NOTES

You can find *pica pau* on fancy menus, but really, there's no need. Find a spit-n-sawdust *tasca*, with FC Porto vs Sporting Lisbon blaring on the TV, and you're good to go. Order a large *pica pau* and some beers and get ready to peck; essential tools are a toothpick to spear the meat, fresh bread to soak up the gravy and a stack of serviettes. A connoisseur might be looking for the right balance of olive oil, pickles and acidity, and a spiciness to make your lips tingle but not enflame. Hungry football fans won't care a fudge – to them, the tender pork, oozy sauce, cold beer, banter and beautiful game are a match made in heaven. ● *by Sarah Baxter*

YOU'LL NEED

Pickling liquid

3 cups (750mL) water
1 cup (250mL) vinegar
2 tbs sugar
1 diced carrot
1 red onion, peeled and
    chopped
½ a leek (white part only),
    chopped
1 bay leaf
3 black peppercorns
3 white peppercorns
8 preserved herring fillets

Mustard sauce

1 tbs sweet (Bavarian) mustard
1 tsp of Dijon mustard
2 tsp sugar
1–2 tbs distilled white vinegar
Pinch of salt
Pinch of freshly ground white
    peppercorns
½ cup chopped dill
¾ cup (185mL) canola oil

ORIGINS

Before oil was discovered in its
waters in the 1960s, Norway was
one of the poorest countries
in Europe; rich in fish and
little else. The Atlantic's vast
schools of herring were so
abundant then that the silvery
fish were a Norwegian staple
for all. Affection for the humble
herring, now a delicacy and far
less abundant, has never waned.
In fact, it's more popular than
ever – not least because
it reminds Norwegians just
how far they've come.

KNAPE; MARCO WONG © GETTY IMAGES. JUSTIN FOULKES © LONELY PLANET IMAGES

SERVES 4 (AS AN ENTRÉE OR APPETISER)

NORWAY

PICKLED HERRING IN MUSTARD SAUCE

Fish for breakfast? Norwegians adore the humble herring, served in vinegar and mustard, so much so that many can't wait until lunchtime for their first fishy fix of the day.

METHOD

1 To make the pickling liquid, combine all the ingredients in a saucepan and bring to the boil. Stir every now and then until the sugar is completely dissolved. Remove from the heat, cover and set aside.

2 Submerge and soak the herring fillets in cold water overnight to remove the saltiness from the fish.

3 Remove the fillets from the water and pat dry with paper towel. Arrange in a shallow baking dish, cover with the pickling brine and refrigerate overnight.

4 To make the mustard sauce, combine the mustards, sugar, vinegar, salt, pepper and dill in a food processor. Drizzle canola oil into the mix in a slow, steady stream until the sauce is thick. Leave in the fridge overnight.

5 The next day, remove the herring from the brine and cut into slices, then serve with the mustard sauce.

TIP *This dish works best if you allow ample time for the fish to soak and marinate – preferably 48 hours. If you can buy the herrings already pickled you'll save yourself a lot of time.*

TASTING NOTES

Let's face it, pickled fish with mustard is an acquired taste – especially at breakfast. And yet, many find themselves repeatedly returning to this pungent favourite, drawn to its tangy strangeness and to the cold, smooth texture of raw, white fish soaked in a zesty mustard and vinegar coating. Find it at the hotel breakfast bar or, like the locals, in one of the open sandwiches that Scandinavians love. Served atop a wedge of bread, you'll most appreciate it sitting by a Norwegian fishing harbour as seabirds whirl and squawk overhead. Here, you'll be surrounded by the invigorating pong of fresh fish and of boat traffic coming and going, as it has along Norway's Atlantic coast for centuries. ● *by Anthony Ham*

ORIGINS

It's virtually impossible to pin down how long this curry has been around. After all, the original curries – a catch-all term for the perplexing array of Asian stews given punch by spices – are thousands of years old. The use of pigs' trotters as the base element probably stems from age-old rural practices that put to use every part of a slaughtered animal. It's a popular festival meal around which to make merry.

YOU'LL NEED

- 1–2 pig trotters (1–1½kg/2–3lb), chopped into large or small pieces according to taste
- 2–3 tbs mustard oil (vegetable oil can be used too)
- 3 onions, peeled and chopped
- ½ tsp ground cumin
- ½ tsp turmeric powder
- 2 tbs ginger and garlic paste (or mince 15 cloves of garlic and 25–50g/1–2oz fresh ginger)
- ½ tsp red chilli powder (mostly for colour, so any red chilli powder will do, such as *Kashmiri mirch* or *Degi mirch*)
- 30 green chilli peppers (for a very spicy curry), halved or diced
- Salt to taste
- 3 tomatoes, chopped
- 2 tbs black mustard seeds, ground (optional)
- 2 tbs lime juice

HIMALAYAN FOOTHILLS (NEPAL, DARJEELING & SIKKIM, INDIA)

PIG TROTTER CURRY

Rare in restaurants but popular for dinner in Himalayan homes, this spicy dish of trotters stewed with vegetables and chilli, known as *khutta ko achaar*, is rooted in Nepali tradition.

METHOD

1 Stir-fry the chopped trotters in a wok or pan until the meat is slightly brown on all sides.

2 In a separate pan, heat the mustard oil. Add the onion and fry until golden brown.

3 Add the ground cumin, turmeric powder, and ginger and garlic paste, and fry until it starts sticking to the pan.

4 Add the red chilli powder, green chillies and salt to taste and fry for about 30 seconds. Note that 30 green chillies will make a very spicy curry; reduce the number of chillies if desired.

5 Add the chopped tomatoes and cook for about 2 minutes.

6 Add the stir-fried trotters to the spices and mix together. Transfer the ingredients to a pressure cooker and cook for around 20 minutes (five or six whistles).

7 While this cooks, roast the ground black mustard seeds in a separate pan.

8 Once the trotters are ready, add the roasted black mustard seeds and the lime juice, then return to the heat for 2 minutes. Serve hot or at room temperature.

TASTING NOTES

The curried-trotter eating experience unfolds in distinct stages. First, the smell is unmistakable – meaty and aromatic, but not overpowering like dishes from northern India. Once the eating has begun, the piquancy of ginger and garlic emerges foremost. Then as you chew into the meat, you'll get a hit of the juicy pork, heightened by the thick gravy of tongue-coating fat and bone marrow. The last blast is enduring chilli, relieved only by the rice or roti accompaniment or a medicinal dose of local *raksi* (sinus-clearing alcohol). This sensory adventure usually takes place in the high-spirited company of a family for whom the trotters are a treat, as is the occasion to share it with a special guest. ● *by Ethan Gelber*

YOU'LL NEED

500g (1lb) fresh Padrón
  peppers, whole
Approx 1 cup (250mL) virgin
  olive oil
Coarse salt to season

ORIGINS

The diminutive peppers made
their way to Spain in the late
16th century, imported as seeds
by Franciscan monks returning
from Mexico. Theories abound
on why some are spicy while
others lack zing. Some say it's
the soil in the valleys around
Padrón, where the peppers are
cultivated, others put it down to
southern Galicia's weather. Most
agree that timing is crucial, with
peppers packing more punch
when harvested in the later
summer months.

SERVES 4

PADRÓN, GALICIA, SPAIN

PIMIENTOS DE PADRÓN

Nine times out of ten, you'll get sweetness and crunch when you bite into these fried whole peppers, but every so often you'll be met with a mouthful of fire.

METHOD

1 Thoroughly rinse the peppers and pat dry with kitchen towel.

2 Heat the oil in a frying pan over a medium heat. You can alter the amount of oil used to suit your tastes but don't be too sparing, the dish is ideally prepared with plenty of oil.

3 Add the peppers to the frying pan in batches, frying for 2–3 minutes on each side.

4 Turn the peppers when they just begin to brown and start to shrivel a little.

5 Once browned all over, place the cooked peppers on to a piece of kitchen towel to drain some of the oil.

6 Transfer to a clean plate and sprinkle with coarse salt.

7 Serve as one of a number of tapas dishes. The peppers can also be served as a side dish for a main meal.

TASTING NOTES

Showcasing a trio of quality ingredients, 'Russian roulette peppers' epitomise authentic, unpretentious Spanish cooking. It's a classic tapa, and a rare vegetarian dish, usually ordered alongside portions of potatoes, meat, seafood and salad. The sweetness of the peppers provides a perfect contrast with the crunch of a coating of rock salt, while the pepper-infused oil left on the plate begs to be mopped up with bread. But the true allure of the peppers is their unpredictability. A simple Galician saying sums up what to expect: 'Os pementos de Padrón – uns pican e outros non' (Padrón peppers – some are hot and some are not); the only way to find out is to shove the whole thing into your mouth. ● *by Lucy Corne*

ORIGINS

Piri-piri sauce is one of the world's original culinary fusions. Reputedly chillies were brought to Europe from the New World by Columbus, then Portuguese navigators exported them to colonies in Africa. Here the fiery bird's-eye chillies were dubbed *pili-pili*, Swahili for 'pepper-pepper', and subsequently cross-pollinated with local African chillies. Eventually, the chillies were transported back to Europe and Portugal, retaining their African name.

SERVES 4

MOZAMBIQUE

PIRI-PIRI CHICKEN

**Flame-grilled chicken marinated in east Africa's most
famous blend of chilli and spices is served oceanside with
a cold beer. The simple things in life are often the best.**

YOU'LL NEED

1 tbs olive oil
4–8 bird's-eye chillies, depending on how hot you want the dish
1½ tsp chopped fresh ginger
4 cloves of garlic, peeled and roughly chopped
½ cup (125mL) lemon juice
1 tbs paprika
1 tsp sea salt
½ tsp pepper
4 chicken legs
Rice or fried potatoes and a fresh green salad to serve

METHOD

1 To make the marinade, combine the olive oil, chillies, ginger, garlic, lemon juice, paprika, salt and pepper in a food processor.

2 Rub the chicken with roughly half the marinade, cover and refrigerate for around 3 hours.

3 After marinating, grill the chicken on a barbecue at medium heat, basting regularly with the remaining marinade until the skin is slightly charred and the juices run clear.

4 Serve with rice or fried potatoes and a fresh green salad.

TASTING NOTES

Sunday afternoon at the beach is a great family tradition in Maputo, Mozambique's capital city. *Futebol* (soccer) games with scores of players on each side swarm up and down the sand, and there's a steady stream of frosty bottles of local 2M ('*Doshem*') lager being retrieved from ice-boxes. In the distance, Maputo's mini-Manhattan emerges from the heat haze and the beach's essential aroma is chicken being grilled with spicy *piri-piri* sauce. If the friendly locals don't ask you to join their barbecues, seek out the busiest of the *piri-piri* stalls punctuating the beach and dive in. Look forward to a smoky flavour combination of chilli heat and citrusy zing, underpinned by expertly grilled chicken with a charred and caramelised skin. ● *by Brett Atkinson*

YOU'LL NEED

1 tsp black peppercorns
1 tsp cumin seeds
2 large plum tomatoes
3 cups (750mL) hot water
1½ tsp salt
2 heaped tbs tamarind paste
3 tbs ghee or canola oil
¼ tsp black mustard seeds
2 medium-sized dried red
  chillies
¼ tsp fenugreek seeds
2 tbs brown sugar
Handful of fresh coriander
  (cilantro) leaves, torn

ORIGINS

As early as AD 1700, South
Indians were witnessed drinking
peppered water, the Tamil
milagu rasam, as a digestif
and were later seen by British
colonialists pouring it over their
rice. Traditionally cooked in an
eeya chombu – a lead vessel
believed to enhance the flavour
– *rasam* continually reinvents
itself with headline ingredients
such as tomato, pineapple,
garlic or lemon.

SOUTH INDIA

RASAM

Revered for its comforting and healing properties, the endlessly versatile *rasam* is South India's 'hot and sour' soup, infused with the exotic herbs and spices so abundant in this region.

TOMATO RASAM

METHOD

1 Using a coffee grinder, or pestle and mortar, grind the peppercorns and cumin seeds until fine, then set aside.

2 Wash and chop the tomatoes and puree with a few tablespoons of water in a food processor. Set aside.

3 Pour the hot water into a soup pot and add the tamarind paste. Bring to the boil, reduce the heat to simmering and add the tomatoes, salt and ground spices. Cook for about 10 minutes.

4 In a heavy saucepan, heat the ghee or oil over a medium heat and fry the mustard seeds until they begin to crackle. Break up the chillies into two or three pieces and add along with the fenugreek seeds. Cook until the seeds release their aromas (1–2 minutes).

5 Add the oil and spices to the soup mixture, along with the brown sugar. Taste and season with more salt or sugar as required.

6 Ladle the soup into bowls and top with torn coriander leaves.

TASTING NOTES

A steaming, aromatic bowl of *rasam* is a wondrous thing for your senses. Amid the pungent smells and cacophony of sweltering Chennai's teeming streets, it will ground you – the intensity of freshly ground peppercorns and tangy tamarind demand attention and tingle your sinuses. Slurping is encouraged – *rasam* is even ladled into cupped hands at festivities such as weddings – but let a mouthful linger for a moment while this deceptively simple broth dazzles your taste buds. Tamarind's bright sourness coupled with a dragonlike burst of heat from pepper and chilli and the subtle nuances of toasted, ground spices never fail to cheer and enliven. ● *by Caroline Veldhuis*

KATE WHITAKER © GETTY IMAGES

ORIGINS

The Arabic term 'ras el hanout' translates as 'head of the shop', an assurance that it's the best your *attar* (spice master) in the souk has to offer. While the ingredients and quantities vary (often carefully guarded secrets), the complex blend can feature up to 50 different spices. There are also rumours that it dates back to biblical times, 'ras', being the title for an Ethiopian king. Intriguingly, there are tales of *attars* customising it with hashish for special clients!

YOU'LL NEED

3 tbs olive oil
2 onions, peeled and thinly sliced
1 tbs finely chopped fresh ginger
1kg (2lb) boneless lamb shoulder, cut in chunks
2 tsp *ras el hanout* (see below for recipe)
2 cinnamon sticks
11/5 cups (300mL) water
800g (1lb 10oz) diced tomatoes
3 bay leaves
Salt and pepper to taste
175g (6oz) dried apricots
Seeds from 1 pomegranate, to serve

Handful of chopped fresh coriander (cilantro) leaves, to serve

Ras El Hanout

½ tsp roasted cardamom seeds
½ tsp roasted fennel seeds
1 tbs roasted coriander seeds
1 tbs roasted cumin seeds
1 tsp cinnamon
1 tsp turmeric
1 tsp cayenne
2 tsp sweet paprika
1 tsp salt
½ tsp sugar
½ tsp allspice
2 whole cloves
¼ tsp ground nutmeg

MOROCCO

RAS EL HANOUT

Slow-cooked, buttery lamb literally melts off the bone, thanks to hours of tenderising in a tagine steaming with aromatic *ras el hanout*, Morocco's trademark mix of numerous spices.

LAMB TAGINE

METHOD

1 Heat the oil in a large, deep casserole dish (or tagine!). Add the onions and saute until soft. Stir in the ginger, add the lamb in portions and fry until lightly coloured. Return all the meat to the pan.

2 Blend/crush the *ras el hanout* ingredients in a mortar and pestle of spice grinder, then add 2 tsp to the lamb. Store the remainder in an airtight jar.

3 Stir in cinnamon sticks and cook for 1 minute. Add the tomatoes and water and bring to a boil, stirring occasionally. Add the bay leaves and salt and pepper to taste, then cover and simmer for about 1½ hours, until the meat is tender.

4 Stir in the apricots and heat for 5 minutes.

5 Serve sprinkled with coriander leaves and pomegranate seeds.

TASTING NOTES

Imagine wandering the labyrinths of Marrakesh with every sense on red alert: the cacophony of buzzy bartering, blaring Arabic music, vibrant kaftan colours, dodging donkeys and snake charmers. The heady aroma of molten lamb penetrates the incense-laden undertow and you veer in the direction of a quiet rooftop for your first taste of authentic tagine. As the terracotta lid is lifted by your host, revel in the steamy, aromatic anticipation. The first nugget of lamb falls apart on your tongue, unctuous with *ras el hanout's* layers of sweet, spicy, warmth, depth. Take a sip of mint tea or perhaps fresh pomegranate juice, tear off some *khobz* (bread) and dive in again. And again. ● *by Karyn Noble*

TOM COCKREM © GETTY IMAGES. JAMES MURPHY PHOTOGRAPHY © CORBIS

YOU'LL NEED

Kerisik
50g (2oz) ground coconut

Spice Paste
6 shallots, peeled
2.5cm (1in) piece of galangal, peeled
2.5cm (1in) piece of ginger, peeled
3 stalks of lemongrass, crushed
4–5 cloves of garlic, peeled
10 dried chillies, soaked in warm water and seeded

Curry
1 tbs oil
1 cinnamon stick
4 cloves
4 star anise
3 cardamom pods
750g (1½lb) lean beef, cut into cubes
1 stalk lemongrass, cut into pieces and crushed
1 cup (250mL) coconut milk
2 tsp tamarind juice
1 cup (250mL) water
6 tbs kerisik
1 tbs palm sugar
6 kaffir lime leaves, finely chopped
Salt to taste
Rice to serve

ORIGINS

Rendang daging was created by the Minangkabau people of West Sumatra, and its ingredients and preparation are said to be a metaphor for the philosophy of *musyawarah* – consultation with elders – that binds Minangkabau society together. The meat is taken to represent the tribal elders, coconut milk represents teachers, poets and writers, chilli represents the guidance of Islam and the spice mix represents the ordinary population, unified by mutual discussion.

SERVES 4

RENDANG DAGING

Thailand can keep its green curry; in Malaysia and Indonesia, *rendang daging* – dry beef curry with roasted coconut and lime leaves in reduced coconut milk – rules the roost.

METHOD

1 To make the *kerisik*, toast the ground coconut in a dry pan until it turns light brown, then blend in a spice mill or mortar and pestle to produce a thick, oily paste.

2 For the spice paste, grind the shallots and other spice ingredients in a blender or mortar and pestle to create a fine paste.

3 For the curry, heat the oil in a pan and add the spice paste, cinnamon, cloves, star anise and cardamom and fry for a minute or so to release the aromas.

4 Add the beef and crushed lemongrass and stir-fry until the meat is browned.

5 Add the coconut milk, tamarind juice and water and simmer until the meat is almost cooked.

6 Add the *kerisik*, palm sugar, kaffir lime leaves and salt to taste, then cover the pan and cook on low heat for 1–1½ hours, until the meat is tender and the liquid has almost all been absorbed.

7 Leave overnight to mature the flavours, then warm and serve with rice.

TASTING NOTES

The slow, labour-intensive preparation of *rending daging* gives this dense, dry curry remarkable properties of preservation – the dish takes half a day to prepare, but can safely be stored for days at room temperature, even in tropical heat. The first surprise when tasting *rending* is how different it is to Thai or Indian curries. The use of roasted coconut gives it a rich, smoky quality more common in Mexican cooking. And while there's plenty of chilli, in *rendang* the heat plays a supporting role, allowing the aromatic herbs and spices – lemongrass, lime leaves, garlic, galangal and ginger – to shine through. Eat it with steamed rice parcels and a big mug of *teh tarik* (Malay 'pulled' tea). ● *by Joe Bindloss*

ORIGINS

Don't be put off by the English name – this is one of those 'lost in translation' moments. What the Chinese name is supposed to suggest is a dish so delicious that you cannot help but start salivating when you think about it – think 'mouth-watering' rather than 'from the chef's mouth'. In Sichuan, it is served hot or cold as a starter to those who can take the heat to stimulate the taste buds for the banquet ahead.

YOU'LL NEED

Poached Chicken
1 fresh chicken, cut into quarters
Pinch of salt
2.5cm (1in) piece fresh ginger, peeled
2 spring onions (scallions), chopped
2 tbs sesame oil

Marinade
2 tbs Sichuan peppercorns
1 clove of garlic, peeled and minced
1 tbs minced fresh ginger
3 tbs dark soy sauce
3 tbs light soy sauce
2 tbs dark vinegar
1 tsp granulated sugar
2 tbs sesame oil
3 tbs chilli oil
40g (1–2oz) roasted peanuts

Garnish
2 tbs sesame seeds
Handful of fresh coriander (cilantro) leaves, chopped

SERVES 4

SICHUAN, CHINA

SALIVA CHICKEN

'Made to make your mouth water' would be a better translation for this searing salad of poached chicken steeped in sesame oil, red chilli oil and lashings of Sichuan pepper.

METHOD

1 Rub the chicken with the salt, then poach it in boiling water in a covered pan with the ginger and spring onions for 20–25 minutes.

2 Turn the chicken and poach for another 20–25 minutes, then transfer to a bowl of cold water and leave to cool. Rub with sesame oil.

3 Bone the chicken quarters and chop the meat into bite-sized pieces.

4 Mix the marinade ingredients together, pour over the chicken and leave to marinate for half an hour.

5 Top the cooked chicken with the garnish and serve.

TASTING NOTES

Despite its potent heat, saliva chicken is remarkably subtle by Sichuan standards. Instead of being an all-out assault on the senses, this is a spicy dish with a sensitive heart. Sure, your first bite will deliver the expected hammer-blow of chilli and Sichuan pepper, but behind that the creaminess of the poached chicken provides a cool, calm place to escape the fire. Each mouthful starts with an explosion but ends with blessed relief. You'll still leave with your lips burning at the end of the meal, but you'll also remember the more subtle flavours in the poached chicken – sesame, coriander and the delicate overtones of ginger and spring onion– a truly mouth-watering combination. ● *by Joe Bindloss*

YOU'LL NEED

1 whole white fish (such as snapper), around 2–2.5kg (4½–5½lb) in size (make sure the fish has been gutted)

Salt

½ cup (125mL) olive oil

5 cloves of garlic, peeled

Handful of finely chopped fresh coriander (cilantro) leaves

1 cup (250mL) tahini

½ cup (125mL) water

½ cup (125mL) lemon juice

½ tsp hot chilli pepper, to taste

2 tbs pinenuts, to serve

ORIGINS

Fish – grilled, baked or, less commonly, fried – has been the essence of eastern Mediterranean cooking for centuries. The fishing fleets of Lebanon and northern Syria, the descendants of the seafaring Phoenicians, long ago placed fish at the heart of the region's culinary traditions. The dish's spices were carried to Arabian ports by traders returning from southern India and Zanzibar, then transported across the deserts of Arabia to the Levant.

LEBANON, SYRIA & JORDAN

SAMAK HARRAH

SERVES 4

Blending Mediterranean subtleties with an uncharacteristically Arabian fiery climax, *samak harrah* is a whole white fish that is fried then baked in its own juices with a selection of spices.

METHOD

1 Pat the fish dry with paper towel or a tea towel, then open two cuts along each side of the fish. Sprinkle salt both inside and out, cover and leave in the fridge for up to 2 hours.

2 Pat the fish dry again, then heat the oil to a high temperature in a large frying pan and fry the fish for 2–3 minutes on each side, but do not cook it through. Place the fish in a lightly oiled baking dish.

3 With a pestle and mortar, grind the garlic, 1 tsp of salt and the coriander until combined.

4 Remove most of the oil from the frying pan before heating again. Add the garlic-coriander mixture and fry until crisp but not burnt. Remove from the heat and allow to cool.

5 Combine the tahini and water while beating it to thicken the consistency. Fold in the lemon juice when thick, then stir in the garlic-coriander mixture and chilli pepper to taste.

6 Pour the mixture over the fish to cover, then bake for 30–35 minutes at 180–200°C (350–200°F). Remove when the fish is cooked through and the sauce is simmering.

7 While the fish is in the oven, gently fry the pine nuts with a little oil until lightly toasted.

8 Sprinkle the fish with the pine nuts and serve.

TIP *This dish is easily prepared at home. Ask your fishmonger to clean and scale the fish to cut back on your own preparation time.*

TASTING NOTES

This dish celebrates an exotic cocktail of flavours from the spice-bearing traditions of the Arabs while also showing fidelity to that great tenet of Mediterranean cooking: take the freshest ingredients and interfere with them as little as possible. The result? A sophisticated balancing act in which the fish cleverly remains star of the show. Garlic and chilli pepper add the fire and bite, while coriander and lemon juice bathe the fish in freshness. Tahini smoothes over their differences with a dense and reassuring texture. Syria may be off-limits but if you eat *samak harrah* in Jordan or Lebanon, the soundtrack to your meal will almost certainly be the mournful strains of an Arabic diva and the *muezzin* call to prayer. ● *by Anthony Ham*

YOU'LL NEED

250g (9oz) carrots, peeled
  and finely chopped
4 tbs oil
1–2 tsp mustard seeds
½ tsp turmeric
2 cloves of garlic, peeled and
  crushed or finely chopped
½–1 green chilli, seeded and
  finely chopped
1 tbs salt
1 tsp caster sugar (optional)
2 tbs lemon or lime juice

ORIGINS

In the 1960s, newly independent
Tanzania's president Julius
Nyerere made a virtue of
agricultural self-sufficiency.
Home-grown vegetables
became a national obsession.
Important for Tanzania's export
earnings are the spices grown
on or imported into Zanzibar,
a key spice hub in ancient times.
Marry the two and you have
carrot sambaro: a symbol of
Tanzania's culinary diversity.

SERVES 4

TANZANIA

SAMBARO

Few African staples add zing to a meal quite like Tanzania's carrot *sambaro*, a dish in which the humble carrot swims in the flavours of the Indian Ocean spice trade.

METHOD

1 Bring to the boil a large pot of water and add the carrots. Boil until the carrots are almost cooked, but still firm. Drain and set aside.

2 In a heavy pan, heat the oil and mustard seeds, stirring so that the oil coats the seeds, then add the turmeric, garlic and chilli. Simmer gently for at least 1 minute.

3 Stir the carrot into the spice mixture until the carrots are coated in the spices, then add the salt and sugar. Cover and allow to simmer gently for 5 minutes.

4 Just as you're about to serve, splash the lemon or lime juice over the carrots.

TIP *This dish is pulled in two directions: one sweet, the other spicy. The latter's influence will depend on which type of mustard seeds you have to hand – black mustard seeds are strongest, white mustard seeds are milder, while the in-between brown mustard seeds will give your dish a hint of Dijon mustard.*

TASTING NOTES

Never have carrots tasted this good! There is an intensity of flavours, each of which is discernible above the whole. Savour the subtle and familiar bite of garlic, the sharper edge of chilli and the aromatic pungency of mustard seeds. Then, to confound everything, you'll be hit by an undercurrent of sugar, giving the dish a moreish quality that makes the next bite irresistible. Tanzanians love to share meals, so *sambaro* is invariably accompanied by much laughter and a cacophony of Swahili. Whether set against a backdrop of traffic noise in Dar es Salaam or the farmyard sounds of rural Tanzania, the effect is the same; one of everyone being welcome as hungry hands dip into the communal pot. ● *by Anthony Ham*

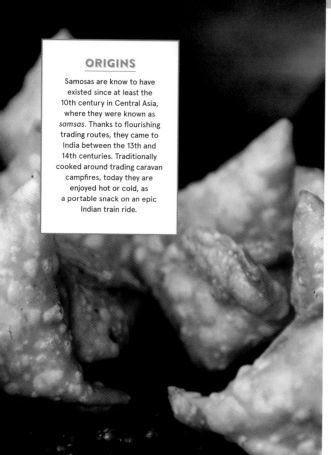

ORIGINS

Samosas are know to have existed since at least the 10th century in Central Asia, where they were known as *samsas*. Thanks to flourishing trading routes, they came to India between the 13th and 14th centuries. Traditionally cooked around trading caravan campfires, today they are enjoyed hot or cold, as a portable snack on an epic Indian train ride.

YOU'LL NEED

Dough
1 cup (150g) plain flour
2 tsp semolina flour
¼ tsp salt
1 tbs vegetable or canola oil
¼ cup (60mL) lukewarm water

Filling
2 tbs vegetable or canola oil
½ tsp cumin seeds
⅓ cup green peas
2 green chillies, seeded and chopped
½ tsp coriander seeds, ground
½ tsp garam masala
2 large potatoes, peeled, boiled and diced (not mashed)
1 tsp *amchur* (mango powder)
Vegetable or canola oil for deep-frying
Chutney to serve

TASTING NOTES

Finding a samosa in India is pretty much a case of following your nose; at the end of the aroma trail, you'll find the samosa *wallah* (vendor) hard at work, preparing his little *maida* (wheat) flour pastry parcels of goodness and dropping them into a sputtering pan of oil. A few flips to cook both sides to golden perfection, and the vendor will scoop out your piping-hot samosa and drop it on to a serving plate with a splodge of tangy mint, coriander or tamarind chutney. Sinking your teeth into the warm, flaky pastry and savouring the blend of spices, coriander, peas, chillies and the soft, yielding texture of the potato is one of the great pleasures of the subcontinent. ● *by Joe Bindloss*

INDIA

SAMOSAS

Forget pasties and pies – the samosa takes the idea of a portable pastry and fills it with a mixture of potatoes, onions, peas, coriander, green chillies and Indian spices.

METHOD

1 To make the dough, combine all the ingredients in a mixing bowl. Knead until the dough is soft, smooth and elastic. Set aside to rest for at least 20 minutes.

2 In a small saucepan, heat the oil and lightly fry the cumin seeds. Add the peas and cook for a couple of minutes, then add the chillies, coriander seeds and garam masala and stir for another couple of minutes.

3 Add the potatoes and gently mix through (so as not to crush the potatoes) until coated in the spices. Stir in the *amchur* and place in a bowl to cool.

4 Lightly knead the dough and divide into two balls. Keep dividing each ball until you end up with eight balls (or 16 if you are making mini-samosas).

5 Using a rolling pin, flatten out the first ball into a circular shape about a millimetre thick and cut the circle in half. Hold one half flat in the palm of your left hand and lightly moisten the edges with water.

6 Fold the semicircle in half and press the straight edges together to form a cone. Stuff this with the filling and close the cone into a triangular shape by pinching and sealing the top edge. Repeat with the rest of the dough.

7 If not using a deep-fryer, heat the oil in a saucepan and test for readiness by dropping in a tiny piece of dough. The oil is ready if the dough sizzles and comes up to the surface gradually. Fry the samosas until golden, a few at a time. Do not overcrowd the pan. Drain on paper towel, then serve with your favourite chutney.

TIP *Making your own pastry for this traditional North Indian vegetarian version is easy and delivers a texture that you simply won't get from the shop-bought variety. You can cook samosas in a deep-fryer, but a heavy-bottomed saucepan will do just as well.*

YOU'LL NEED

3 tbs olive oil
1 large onion, peeled and chopped
2 cloves of garlic, peeled and minced
3 red capsicums, diced
1 red chilli, chopped
2 tsp caraway seeds
750g (1½lb) fresh tomatoes, peeled, seeded and chopped (tinned tomatoes can be substituted)
2–3 tsp paprika
1 tsp ground cumin
1 tsp sea salt
1–2 tbs harissa (optional)
4 large eggs
Fresh crusty bread to serve

ORIGINS

Some claim it was introduced to North Africa by the Ottoman Turks, but *shakshouka* is commonly acknowledged as being Tunisian in origin. It's certainly likely that in Israel, where the dish is enormously popular, *shakshouka* first arrived thanks to the immigration of Tunisian Jews in the mid-20th century. It's a simple concept, remarkably similar to Mexican *huevos rancheros*.

SERVES 4

TUNISIA

SHAKSHOUKA

Essentially eggs poached in a molten mound of spicy tomato stew that comes in many different variations, *shakshouka* is the ultimate wake-me-up throughout North Africa and the Middle East.

METHOD

1 Heat the oil to a medium-sized frying pan over medium-high heat. Saute the onion and garlic for about 5 minutes, until soft.

2 Add the capsicum, chilli and caraway seeds. Saute until the capsicum is tender (about 5 minutes).

3 Add the tomatoes, paprika, cumin, salt and harissa (if using). Bring to a boil then reduce the heat to medium-low and cook, stirring occasionally, for about 15 minutes.

4 Make shallow wells in the sauce for the eggs (you can use the back of a spoon). Carefully break in the eggs.

5 Cover the pan and cook the eggs over a low heat. For soft yolks, allow around 5 minutes. If you wish, you can swirl the sauce into the egg whites as they cook, being careful not to damage the yolks.

6 Serve with fresh crusty bread.

TASTING NOTES

Who needs coffee when spice can get the synapses firing in the morning? *Shakshouka* is a visual treat as well as a savoury one – try making it yourself to watch the eggs turn opaque and start googling up at you from the pan. But don't break the yolks! That's a pleasure to reserve for the eating: experience the gradual merging of tastes as the wholesome, rich yolk mixes with its spicy surrounds, cutting through the acidity while taking on all the pep of the chillies and paprika. Be sure to have some fresh, crusty bread on the side; use it to mix the colours, textures and delightful flavours of this warming, invigorating dish. ● *by Kate Whitfield*

SERVES 4

ORIGINS

This is a dish born in celebration. In traditional times, the festivities might have been to mark a successful hunt, one that brought the rare treat of gazelle meat into the camp of semi-nomadic Bedouin. Or it might have been to consolidate a treaty between once-warring tribes, pacts sealed over a meal eaten from a communal bowl. Today, *shawayuh* is the centrepiece of extended family gatherings; a reminder of Yemen's links to an Arabian past.

YEMEN

SHAWAYUH

The essence of Bedouin hospitality and steeped in tradition, *shawayuh* is meat sprinkled with some *hawaij* (a blend of peppercorns, caraway seeds, saffron, cardamom and turmeric) then flame-licked over charcoal.

YOU'LL NEED

4 large grilling steaks or lamb chops
3 tsp *hawaij* (see below)
10 tbs olive oil
Salt to taste

Hawaij
5–6 tsp black peppercorns
2–3 tsp caraway seeds
1 tsp saffron threads
1 tsp cardamom seeds
2 tsp turmeric

METHOD

1 To make the *hawaij* mix, grind the peppercorns, caraway seeds, saffron threads and cardamom seeds until blended together. Stir in the turmeric and store in a sealed jar.

2 Coat the meat all over with the *hawaij* mix and set aside for 30 minutes.

3 When your coals are red hot, very lightly coat the meat in the oil and position over the fire. Once seared, turn the meat over and repeat on the other side.

4 When evenly seared, move the meat to a cooler part of the fire and leave until cooked to your preference. You may need to apply light brushes of oil throughout the cooking.

5 Season with salt and serve.

TIP *The only way to replicate the traditional way of cooking this dish is over the hot coals of a barbecue or an open fire. When cooked in other ways, you'll miss the charcoal smell and taste that permeate the meat and are the essence of the dish.*

TASTING NOTES

Shawayuh is the taste of the open fire as the meat's smoky flavour lingers on the tongue. The piquant *hawaij* seasoning enhances the experience in subtle ways, through a sharp bite from the peppercorn, a hint of saffron and the aromatic suggestion of humid tropical coasts in the combination of cardamom and turmeric. It is a dish that tastes best shared with family and community; individual portions may be cut and distributed, but tradition demands that the meat be placed in the centre of the table (or, better still, a picnic blanket alongside the open fire) and torn off in chunks with bare hands. Imagine a soundtrack of locals telling tall tales in guttural Arabic and the meal is complete. ● *by Anthony Ham*

YOU'LL NEED

300g (11oz) dried rice noodles

2 tsp madras (hot) curry powder

1 tsp ground turmeric

3 tbs light soy sauce

2 tbs rice wine or sherry

½ cup (125mL) chicken stock or water

Vegetable oil for stir-frying

3 medium eggs, beaten

150g (5oz) medium raw prawns

100g (3½oz) chicken breast, sliced into strips

100g (3½oz) *char siu* pork, sliced thinly

1 clove of garlic, peeled and crushed

2cm (¾in) piece of ginger, grated

1 medium red chilli, chopped

4 spring onions (scallions), chopped

1 small green capsicum, sliced thinly

150g (5oz) bean sprouts

Chopped spring onions (scallions) and coriander (cilantro) to garnish

Lime wedges to serve

ORIGINS

Singapore noodles' history is elusive, but it definitely is *not* from Singapore. A common belief is that Cantonese chefs invented it to reflect multicultural influences. Given its popularity in countries like the UK and the USA, a more likely beginning involves Western chefs attempting to replicate the fusion flavours of Singapore-style noodles, such as *char kway teow* (from China) and *mee goreng* (Indian/Malay origins).

CHINA (HONG KONG), UK, US, CANADA, AUSTRALIA
(EVERYWHERE BUT SINGAPORE!)

SINGAPORE NOODLES

A tantalising blend of subtle curry and oriental flavours and a surf-and-turf combination of pork and prawns make Singapore noodles a winning fusion of East and West.

METHOD

1 Soak the noodles in boiling water for a few minutes until soft, then drain the water and set aside.

2 Make the sauce by combining the curry powder, turmeric, soy sauce, rice wine or sherry and chicken stock in a small bowl.

3 Put a teaspoon of oil in a wok on medium-high heat, scramble the eggs then take them out of the wok and set aside.

4 Add a little more oil. Sear, but do not cook, the prawns and set aside.

5 Add a little more oil if necessary, cook the chicken and set aside.

6 Put a tablespoon of oil in the wok, then quickly fry the garlic, ginger, chilli and spring onions for a few minutes.

7 Add the sauce and the capsicum and heat until the sauce is simmering.

8 Toss in the noodles, stirring to coat, then return the prawns, chicken and egg to the wok and add the pork and bean sprouts. Stir-fry for a few minutes.

9 Garnish with the spring onions and coriander. Serve immediately with lime wedges.

TIP *Have all your ingredients prepared and ready to go in the wok for fast cooking. Feel free to use more or less chilli according to taste.*

TASTING NOTES

A complete meal in itself, nothing beats Singapore noodles when you have a craving for a savoury, protein-laden, moreish treat. The dish is an explosion of flavours and textures – smoky curry provides plenty of oomph to soft chicken and crunchy prawns, balanced by the sweet *char siu* and crispy vegetables. Golden-hued noodles, green capsicum and deep-red pork also make for a veritable feast for the eyes. This cheap and filling dish is found everywhere from street food stalls to teahouses, restaurants and everything in between, not to mention being a cinch to cook at home. Variations include the addition of cabbage, mushrooms or sesame oil. ● *by Johanna Ashby*

ORIGINS

The prototype for *som tam* – which translates to 'pounded sour' – almost certainly came from Laos, but it was the Thais, more specifically the chefs serving generations of backpackers in Bangkok, who put the dish on the international menu. Even today, the version served in Bangkok is celebrated as the fieriest, thanks to the addition of an extra-generous handful of bird's-eye chillies in the pounded green papaya, lime juice, fish sauce, palm sugar and dried shrimp mixture.

SERVES 4 AS A SIDE DISH

THAILAND & LAOS

SOM TAM

**Think green papaya salad is nothing to be scared of?
Think again. To create *som tam*, papaya is pounded with
raw bird's-eye chillies, creating a dressing that can strip paint.**

YOU'LL NEED

½ green papaya
3–4 cloves of garlic, peeled
  and crushed
4–5 raw bird's-eye chillies,
  crushed
3 tomatoes, cut into wedges
225g (8oz) bean sprouts
150g (5oz) yard long beans,
  chopped
50g (2oz) dried shrimp
50g (2oz) roasted peanuts,
  chopped, to garnish

Dressing
Juice from 1 lime
2–3 tbs fish sauce
2 tbs palm sugar

METHOD

1 Cut the green papaya in half, then remove the seeds and grate the flesh into thin strips.

2 Add the green papaya to a large mortar and pestle with the garlic and chillies and pound to release the flavours.

3 Add the chopped tomatoes, bean sprouts, yard long beans and dried shrimp, then top with the dressing ingredients.

4 Mix roughly in the mortar and pestle. Garnish with chopped peanuts and serve.

TASTING NOTES

Before you taste *som tam*, you get to enjoy the theatre of its preparation. First comes the shredding of the green papaya, then the pounding, as ingredients are thrashed to within an inch of their lives in an earthenware mortar and pestle. Atomised chilli is already thick in the air when the dish is served, and the only option once you start is to keep on going, consuming every delicious mouthful before the awful reality of how much raw chilli you are eating starts to dawn. But what flavours! *Som tam* is at once tart, sour, sweet, salty, pungent and fresh. Eating is followed by a lengthy phase of panting and wishing there was something to take away the burn! ● *By Joe Bindloss*

ORIGINS

Souse has its origin with the West African slaves brought to the Caribbean to work the plantations of Barbados, Trinidad, Saint Kitts and other islands. It is inspired by English 'head cheese' – loose patés made of leftover meat bits – modified to the local climate to be a cold soup, rather than a solid. Slave cooks worked with what they had, which was often the parts of the pig thrown out by the masters.

SERVES 4

CARIBBEAN ISLANDS

SOUSE

What's the world's best hangover cure? A Caribbean native would name this cold spicy soup made from pickled pork trotters, head and tail. Don't knock it till you've tried it.

YOU'LL NEED

500g (1lb) ham hocks

2 cloves of garlic, peeled and crushed

½ medium red onion, peeled and thinly sliced

Juice of 4 limes

Black pepper to taste

1 Scotch bonnet chilli (or 2 jalapeño chillies), thinly sliced

1 tsp salt

1 cucumber, thinly sliced

Large handful of fresh coriander (cilantro) leaves, chopped

4 cups (1L) water

METHOD

1 Wash the ham hocks and place them in a large pot with water (enough to cover the meat) along with the garlic.

2 Bring to the boil, then reduce to a simmer and cook until tender – about 2 hours.

3 Drain the meat and set it aside to cool.

4 Once cooled, shred the meat and toss it with the lime juice and black pepper.

5 Add the remaining ingredients and water, and allow to marinate for several hours.

6 Serve cold.

TASTING NOTES

Souse is a weekend treat throughout much of the Caribbean. You'll find it served for Saturday lunch, along with its traditional accompaniment – blood pudding. In some countries, the pudding is more like a sausage, savoury black blood flecked with soft rice. In others, such as Barbados, the pudding is made from sweet potatoes darkened to look like blood pudding, without any actual blood. On weekends, souse-lovers queue up outside the homes of popular souse-makers, waiting for their hit of cool, spicy, salty, porky broth. Line up with them, eat your souse standing in the front yard, then return the bowl. You'll also find a big tureen of souse at any Caribbean festival or dance party, alongside the rum. ● *By Emily Matchar*

YOU'LL NEED

2 cups (500mL) coconut milk
500g (1lb) sliced chicken,
    pork, seafood or tofu
100g (3½oz) eggplants
100g (3½oz) pea eggplants
2 tsp palm sugar
2 kaffir lime leaves
Fish sauce to taste
3–5 red chillies, seeded, finely
    sliced
1 cup fresh Thai sweet basil
    leaves
Jasmine rice to serve

Paste

20 Thai green chillies
2 tbs galangal, chopped
6 tbs lemongrass, white
    portion, scraped and
    chopped
2 kaffir lime leaves
4 pieces coriander root,
    chopped
1 tsp chopped red turmeric
4 shallots, peeled and
    chopped
4 cloves of garlic, peeled and
    chopped
1 tsp shrimp paste

ORIGINS

Each Southeast Asian country
has its own variation of curry.
Thailand has many – red,
panang, massaman, yellow,
sour and green. During the
Ayutthaya period (AD 1351–1767),
Siam opened its borders to
trade, allowing in the Indians
and Moors who are said to have
added milk and/or cream to the
local spice pastes. Through the
years, the cream was replaced
with coconut cream. The rest
is (food) history.

SERVES 4

THAILAND

THAI GREEN CURRY

A zesty blend of green chillies and spices cooked in coconut milk and coconut cream along with meat or seafood and vegetables, green curry is quintessential Thai comfort food.

METHOD

1 Pound the paste ingredients in a pestle and mortar until well mixed. Set aside.

2 Heat a large saucepan or wok and add the cream from the top of the coconut milk (don't shake the can before opening it).

3 Stir the cream. When it has split, add the curry paste and fry with the cream until it's fragrant. Add the remaining coconut milk.

4 Add your meat, seafood or tofu and bring the mixture to a boil. Simmer for 5–10 minutes.

5 Add the eggplants, pea eggplants, palm sugar and kaffir lime leaves to the curry and simmer for another 2 minutes, stirring occasionally.

6 Add fish sauce for saltiness and chillies for spice. Boil through and stir in the basil leaves for a minute more before serving with jasmine rice.

TASTING NOTES

Yes, the colour comes from the chillies! But along with zingy Thai green chillies, green curry paste is made from a bunch of other fresh ingredients: lemongrass, kaffir lime leaves and liquorice-flavoured sweet Thai basil. During cooking, coconut cream and coconut milk are added to soften the spicy edge, and fish sauce provides umami (savoury flavour). True gourmands will seek out a restaurant that serves this curry spicy, with an oily sheen on top – from oil that splits from the coconut cream. The versatility of this dish explains much of its universal popularity – it's just as tasty with seafood as it is with chicken or pork. Vegetarians can add more eggplant and tofu for a tasty, protein-filled meal. ● *By Shawn Low*

YOU'LL NEED

4 chicken thighs, boned, skinned, diced

Marinade

2 bunches of fresh coriander (cilantro), leaves only
½ cup (125mL) full-fat natural yoghurt
4 fresh green chillies
½ tsp salt
2.5cm (1in) piece of fresh ginger, peeled
4 cloves of garlic, peeled

Masala sauce

1 cinnamon stick
2 cloves
3 red chillies, minced
Vegetable oil
1 onion, peeled and chopped
3 cloves of garlic, peeled
2.5cm (1in) piece of fresh ginger, peeled and grated
½ tsp ground ginger
½ tsp ground cumin
½ tsp ground coriander
½ tsp ground turmeric
½ tsp ground fenugreek
1 tsp hot chilli powder
1 tin (400g/14oz) chopped tomatoes
1¼ cups (400mL) water
½ cup (125mL) single cream
½ tsp sugar
½ tsp salt

ORIGINS

The roots of chicken tikka can be traced back to the Punjab, and the 16th-century court of Babur. The ruler couldn't abide bones in his food, so his cooks pulled the meat into pieces to remove them. But the masala magic wasn't added (allegedly) until the 1970s. After a complaint about the dryness of the chicken, it's said that Ali Ahmed Aslam – owner of Glasgow's Shish Mahal restaurant – created a sauce using spices and condensed tomato soup.

SERVES 2

UNITED KINGDOM

TIKKA MASALA

Its roots might be Indian but the heartland of this creamy baked curry lies further west. Tikka masala has become a national treasure, and an edible exemplification of multicultural Britain.

METHOD

1 Blend the marinade ingredients into a paste; pour over the chicken and leave for at least 2 hours.

2 Fry the cinnamon, cloves and minced chilli in the oil for 1 minute. Add the onion and fry until soft.

3 Blend the garlic and ginger to a paste and add to the onions.

4 Add the ground spices and chilli powder and cook for 5 minutes.

5 Stir in the tomatoes and water, and cook until reduced by half. Leave to cool slightly,

then transfer to a blender and process to a smooth paste.

6 Return to the pan. Off the heat, stir in the cream, sugar and salt, the return the pan to the heat.

7 Grill the chicken until it cooked through and slightly charred.

8 Toss the cooked chicken in the pan with the sauce.

TIP *Marinade the chicken for several hours for the tastiest tikka.*

TASTING NOTES

The classic curry-house experience is usually scoffed after a night on the town. It goes like this: first, you destroy a pile of poppadoms and a cold Indian beer. Then the tikka masala arrives – a vibrant-red vision, so bright it glows. It feels like cheating – amid the *phaals* and *vindaloos*, this is the soft option, a creamy treat rather than a fiery challenge. But, so what? You value your bowels and taste buds, and would prefer your head not blown off, thanks very much. Plus, it looks so good: chunks of marinated chicken enveloped in velvety sauce, pungent with ginger, garlic and spices. And, with rice and naans, it's ideal for soaking up the excesses of the night. ● *By Sarah Baxter*

ORIGINS

Ubiquitous across the Malay Peninsula, *tom yam* is a fiery palate-cleanser that is served everywhere from Thailand and Laos to Malaysia and Singapore. Prawns have been farmed in Thai creeks for centuries, so the dish may have its roots far from the sea, but liberal use of chilli dates *tom yam* to after the 17th century, when the first ones were transported to Southeast Asia from South America by Portuguese seafarers.

YOU'LL NEED

3 cups (750mL) fish or chicken stock
4 cloves of garlic, peeled and crushed
5 shallots, peeled and thinly sliced
2 stalks of lemongrass, cut into 2.5cm (1in) slices
4 thin slices of galangal
200g (7oz) straw mushrooms, sliced lengthways
10 bird's-eye chillies, cut lengthways
3 tbs fish sauce
5 kaffir lime leaves
250g (9oz) raw prawns, washed, peeled and de-veined
Juice from 1 lime
Handful of chopped fresh coriander (cilantro) leaves to garnish

🌶🌶🌶 DISHES

SERVES 4

THAILAND

TOM YAM GUNG

Take fresh prawns, straw mushrooms and stock, add one
part lemongrass, one part lime and one part napalm and
serve – Thailand's favourite soup is a chilli-laced masterpiece.

METHOD

1 In a pan or wok, bring the stock to the boil,
then add the garlic, shallots, lemongrass
and galangal.

2 Add the straw mushrooms, chillies, fish
sauce and kaffir lime leaves.

3 Return to the boil for 2–3 minutes, then add
the prawns and cook until just done.

4 Remove the pan from the heat and add the
lime juice, then stir and serve, garnishing each
portion with chopped coriander.

TASTING NOTES

Floating pools of red chilli oil provide the first warning that something fiery lurks beneath
the surface of this seafood soup. Vapours of lemongrass, galangal and lime rise up,
promising a visceral tour through the flavours of Southeast Asia. The first sensation is the
tang of lime but, almost immediately, the chilli takes control. This is a dish to eat quickly,
without pausing, in case the fire proves too powerful to quench. The main ingredients –
prawns and mushrooms – are secondary to the complex take-no-prisoners blend of
spices and seasonings. Each takes its own moment to shine; some spoonfuls dominated
by lemongrass and lime, others by chilli and medicinal notes of galangal. Keep tissues
to hand... ● *By Joe Bindloss*

ORIGINS

The story goes that a hungry man from Guadalajara came home after a long day of work. All there was for dinner was a piece of old bread, some leftover beans and a couple of pieces of cooked pork. That made for a boring *torta*, so he reached for the spicy salsa his wife had cooked and submerged the whole *torta* in the salsa. Now, he was on to something...

YOU'LL NEED

About 30 dried *chiles de árbol*, stemmed and seeded
¾ cup (185mL) cider vinegar
2 tbs pumpkin seeds, toasted
1½ tbs sesame seeds, toasted
1 tsp dried oregano
1 tsp kosher salt or sea salt
¼ tsp ground cumin
⅛ tsp ground allspice
⅛ tsp ground cloves
2 cloves of garlic, peeled
¾ cup (185mL) water
1 crusty bread roll
1½ cups shredded leftover roasted pork shoulder
¼ small yellow onion, peeled and thinly sliced
1 radish, thinly sliced

TASTING NOTES

Connoisseurs insist that what makes a great *torta ahogada* is a good *birote*, the region's crusty, salty bread that is able hold the contents AND to retain its crunch in spite of being drowned in salsa. Those new to the *torta* may consider asking for it only 'half-drowned', which means the spicy salsa is diluted with plain tomato salsa. On street stalls in Guadalajara they will serve you this street-food favourite in a bowl, along with a spoon and a handful of pickled onions. You can eat it with the spoon, which gets awkward, or with your hands, which get messy, so most people roll up their sleeves and eat it standing up, holding it away from their bodies. ● *By Mauricio Velázquez de León*

GUADALAJARA, MEXICO

TORTAS AHOGADAS

Tortas are widespread throughout Mexico, but only in Guadalajara do these pork-and-bean 'Mexican sandwiches' take a dip into a fiery salsa to become a real – drowned – torta ahogada.

METHOD

1 Combine the chillies, vinegar, pumpkin and sesame seeds, oregano, salt, cumin, allspice, cloves and garlic in a blender and puree until very smooth.

2 Pour through a medium strainer into a bowl, discard any solids and stir in the water. This is the *chile de árbol* sauce.

3 Heat the oven to 180°C (350°F).

4 Split the roll and fill the bottom half with pork.

5 Place on a baking sheet and bake until warmed through and the bread is toasted, about 6 minutes.

6 Add the onion and radish and the top bun; pour *chile de árbol* sauce over the sandwich, and let it sit, so that the sauce soaks in.

ORIGINS

The first recorded *tteokbokki* recipe appeared in a 19th-century cookbook, but as a dish served at the royal courts it dates back much further (it gets a mention in a medical book from around AD 1460). Through the years there have been many incarnations but the current 'street' version was first made in 1953. The Korean War had ended, Seoul was recovering and a lady named Ma Bok-rim started selling *tteokbokki* out of Sindang-dong as cheap comfort food.

YOU'LL NEED

500g (1lb) *tteokbokki tteok* (rice cakes)

100g (3½lb) *eomuk* (fish cake), sliced

150g (5oz) cabbage, chopped

2 spring onions (scallions), chopped

2 cloves of garlic, peeled and finely chopped

1 tsp sesame oil

1 tsp sesame seeds (optional)

Sauce

3 cups (750mL) anchovy stock (from stock powder) or water

3 tbs *gochujang* (red chilli paste)

1 tbs *gochugaru* (red chilli pepper flakes) or regular chilli flakes

1 tbs soy sauce, plus additional to taste

1 tbs sugar, plus extra to taste

NOTE *These ingredients are all available at Asian or Korean grocers.*

SERVES 4

KOREA

TTEOKBOKKI

A dish of rice cakes soaked in a fiery fermented red chilli sauce, *tteokbokki* (tot-pok-ki) was once served in Korea's royal courts, but is now a humble street snack.

METHOD

1 For the sauce: pour the anchovy stock or water into a medium-sized pan. Add the sauce ingredients and bring to a boil. Make sure the paste is dissolved. Reduce the heat to medium.

2 Add the rice cakes and boil until soft (roughly 7–10 minutes).

3 Reduce to a simmer to thicken the sauce. Keep stirring to prevent the rice cakes from burning on the bottom of the pan.

4 Add the fish cakes, cabbage, spring onions and garlic.

5 Simmer for an additional 5 minutes.

6 Season to taste with additional sugar and soy sauce, bearing in mind that the *gochujang* itself is salty.

7 Add the sesame oil, stir through and dish out in bowls. Top with sesame seeds if desired.

TASTING NOTES

Fodder for kings and officials, the original dish was chock-full of the good stuff: vegetables, meat, gingko nuts and walnuts. The modern street version has little by way of nutrition, yet the masses love it, and it's easy to see the appeal: Koreans rock up to street carts and are served up a steaming plate of *tteokbokki*, often to share. Stick your skewer into one of the cylindrical rice cakes, pop it in your mouth and you'll be hit with a multitude of flavours. The saltiness of the fermented soy bean, the kick of the red chillies and the chewy texture... it's magically warming in winter. Be sure to have a cold drink standing by to douse the flames! ● *By Shawn Low*

YOU'LL NEED

2 large onions, peeled and
  sliced
2 tbs cooking oil
4 tbs vinegar
1 tsp brown sugar
1 tsp mustard seeds
1 tbs finely chopped garlic
1 tbs finely chopped fresh
  ginger
1 tbs ground coriander
¼ tsp turmeric powder
Salt to taste
1kg (2lb) pork, cut into bite-
  sized pieces
1½ cups (375mL) of water
Steamed rice or warm naan
  to serve

Masala Paste

¾ tsp roasted fenugreek
  seeds
1 tsp roasted cumin seeds
1 tsp peppercorns
6–8 dried chillies, lightly
  roasted
4cm (1¼in) stick of cinnamon
2 cardamom pods
2 tsp of water

ORIGINS

Vindaloo is derived from a
traditional Portuguese dish
called *carne vinha de alhos* –
literally 'meat with wine and
garlic' – but the dish underwent
a subcontinental makeover with
palm vinegar, spices and chillies
when the Portuguese ruled
the coast of Goa as a colony
for almost five centuries until
1961. An Anglicised version of
vindaloo reigns in British Indian
restaurants, but the authentic
sweet, sour version is best eaten
in Panjim's backstreets in Goa.

GOA, INDIA

VINDALOO

SERVES 4–6

Often bearing an (undeserved) reputation for extreme heat, a Goanese *vindaloo* is a surprisingly subtle and complex dish that showcases culinary echoes of colonialism across the centuries.

PORK VINDALOO

METHOD

1 Saute the chopped onions in 1 tbs of cooking oil until caramelised. Using a blender, blitz the onion mixture until it becomes a paste and set aside.

2 Combine the vinegar and brown sugar and set aside.

3 Fry the mustard seeds in the pan you used for the onions until they sizzle, then add the chopped garlic and ginger and fry for another 2 minutes.

4 Mix in the ground coriander, turmeric powder and salt. Add the pork pieces and fry for around 6–8 minutes until they have browned. Remove and set aside.

5 Make your masala paste by blitzing all the paste ingredients together in a blender or pestle and mortar.

6 In your original pan, add the remaining oil and stir-fry the chopped onion paste and the masala paste for 2 minutes. Stir in the vinegar and sugar mixture and the water.

7 Add the browned pork pieces, and cook until the meat softens and a thick gravy is formed. Serve with steamed rice or warm naan.

TASTING NOTES

Although a dish with a reputation for extreme heat – largely from its popularity in British curry houses – *vindaloo* in Goa is more subtle and balanced. A one-dimensional British *vindaloo* is prepared with a heavy hand on the chilli, but in Goa the dish's historic roots are more evident. Imparting a distinctive sourness, palm vinegar and garlic replaces the wine vinegar and garlic infusion the Portuguese used to preserve pork on sea voyages. The all-important masala spices – fenugreek, cumin, roasted chilli, cinnamon, peppercorns and cardamom – are layered and distinct, their individual flavours released as essential oils during slow-roasting. Finally, there's an earthy sweetness from the addition of sugar and ginger. Mop it up with rice or naan. ● *By Brett Atkinson*

ORIGINS

The model for this supercharged salad was *yam yang nam tok*, aka 'waterfall beef', from Isarn province in northeast Thailand. The waterfall in question is juices dripping from the grilled beef, which blend with lime juice, fish sauce and palm sugar to form a spontaneous dressing for the fragrant coriander and mint leaves and punchy sliced shallots and chillies. It's as refreshing as an early morning dip in the Andaman Sea and as fiery as a blast furnace.

SERVES 4

THAILAND

YAM NEUA

A creation worthy of a celebrity chef, *yam neua* blends grilled beef with Thai herbs, lime juice, palm sugar, fish sauce and lashings of chilli. This is salad for grown-ups!

YOU'LL NEED

400g (14oz) sirloin steak
1 tbs vegetable oil
Salt and pepper to taste
Juice from 1 lime
4 tbs fish sauce
1 tbs palm sugar
10 bird's-eye chillies, cut lengthways
3 cloves of garlic, peeled and thinly sliced
5 shallots, peeled and sliced
Large handful of mint leaves
Large handful of fresh coriander (cilantro) leaves, coarsely chopped
1 small cucumber, thinly sliced

METHOD

1 Rub the meat with vegetable oil, salt and pepper and then grill over high heat in an iron pan to medium rare.

2 Remove from the heat and slice the steak thinly with a sharp knife and set aside.

3 Mix the lime juice, fish sauce and palm sugar in a small bowl, then add the chillies and garlic and set aside.

4 Mix the shallots, mint leaves, coriander leaves, cucumber and beef slices together in a serving bowl, stir in the dressing and serve.

TASTING NOTES

Whenever you take salad beyond the realms of sliced vegetables, you know something special is going to happen. *Yam neua* is less a side salad than a roast dinner served on a bed of fresh herbs, with a secret chilli payload that will have steam coming out of your ears. As you bite into the first mouthful, fresh herbs and lime juice mingle on the palate, but it only takes a second for the raw power of the chillies and shallots to punch through. Eating *yam neua* is an exquisite balance of pleasure and pain caused by those contradictory Thai tastes – hot and sour, sweet and salt – that sound so wrong, but taste so right. ● *By Joe Bindloss*

ORIGINS

Sichuan food may have started as a favourite cuisine of China's royal dynasties who settled in Sichuan province, but it's now popular local fare, with plenty of well-known favourites, such as twice-cooked pork, spicy tofu with minced pork, and dry-fried green beans. The name *yu xiang qie zi*, which translates to 'fish-fragrant' eggplant, is likely to have originated from the Sichuanese's love of cooking fish and the use of classic Sichuanese ingredients.

YOU'LL NEED

2 tbs vegetable oil
4 medium-sized eggplants, chopped into bite-sized cubes
2 cloves of garlic, peeled and crushed
1 tbs grated fresh ginger
1 tsp Sichuan pepper, ground
Handful of dried whole chillies
Chopped spring onions (scallions) to garnish
Steamed rice to serve

Sauce

1 tbs chilli bean paste
2 tbs soy sauce
2 tbs Chinese black vinegar (balsamic vinegar can be used as a substitute)
1 tbs rice wine or dry sherry
1 tsp sugar
1 tsp cornstarch

SERVES 6

CHINA

YU XIANG QIE ZI

Curiously named 'fish-fragrant' eggplant, this stir-fried eggplant
in chilli bean sauce mixed with Chinese black vinegar displays the
hallmarks of classic Sichuanese cuisine – hot, sour, sweet and salty.

METHOD

1 Prepare the sauce by combining the chilli
bean paste, soy sauce, vinegar, rice wine
or sherry, sugar and cornstarch in a bowl.
Set aside.

2 Heat the oil in a wok and add the eggplant.
Fry for a few minutes then add a couple
of tablespoons of water and cook until the
eggplant is golden brown and soft.

3 Add the garlic, ginger, pepper and chillies
and cook for 2–3 minutes until fragrant.

4 Stir in the sauce to coat the eggplant and
simmer until the sauce starts to thicken.

5 Garnish with the spring onions and serve
immediately with just-steamed rice.

TASTING NOTES

There's not much to fish-fragrant eggplant, other than cubes of eggplant quickly wok-fried
in a thick sauce of fermented soybeans in chilli sauce, black vinegar, garlic, ginger, Sichuan
peppercorns and lots of dried chillies – yet it packs an unbelievably invigorating and dynamic
punch. Perfect for soaking up strong flavours, the humble eggplant is tossed until soft and
golden and then doused in a fiery and aromatic blend of traditional Sichuanese spices. The
result is a balanced carnival of hot, sour, sweet and salty. The meatiness of the eggplant
means it can stand on its own or as part of a multi-course banquet, eaten with rice and
drowned with cold beer to offset the fiery nature of the dish. ● *By Joe Bindloss*

ORIGINS

Zahtar (also spelled *za'atar*) is both a dish in itself and a herb plant, the purifying properties of which were revered in Roman times and in Ancient Israel under King David. In both manifestations, zahtar resonates through Arab society as a symbol of home and homeland: it is a reassuring element of one's deep roots in the land, but also, in the case of the Palestinians, a symbol of longing for homelands lost.

SERVES 6

IRAN & PALESTINE

ZAHTAR

This tasty yet underrated Middle Eastern dip is an intensely flavoured spice-and-nuts combo, a staple of Iraqi and Palestinian cuisines and a signifier of how these nations see themselves.

YOU'LL NEED

150g (5oz) sesame seeds
60g (2oz) coriander seeds
90g (3oz) walnuts
Salt and pepper to taste
1½ tbs cumin powder
¾ tbs cinnamon powder
¾ tbs sumac powder
Arab flatbread and olive oil
   to serve

METHOD

1 Toast the sesame seeds under the grill or in a dry frying pan until they begin to pop and turn golden. Do the same for the coriander seeds and then the walnuts.

2 Using a pestle and mortar, crush the seeds and nuts into a powder (but don't pulverise the mixture).

3 Add the salt and pepper and the remaining spices and mix well.

4 To eat, dip the bread first in the oil, then in the *zahtar*.

TIP *Sumac powder (a citrus-tinged spice) is widely available from Asian or multicultural grocery stores; in some countries you'll even find it in mainstream stores. Store leftovers in an air-tight jar and they will keep.*

TASTING NOTES

The texture of *zahtar* will be unusual for those expecting a smooth, hummus-like dip. Its consistency is more powdery than creamy, which is why unctuous olive oil is as much an essential component as the *khoubz* (Arab flatbread), to soak up the powder and alleviate the dryness. Cinnamon, cumin and coriander contribute to a sweetness that is invariably the first impression. But there's also a hint of sourness that lingers, thanks to the deep-red berries of the sumac bush. Walnuts add a trace of bitterness for good measure. In this dish's heartland of Iraq and the Palestinian Territories, the soulful stringed oud, earnest conversation about politics and the arts, and Arab pop music would undoubtedly accompany your eating experience. ● *By Anthony Ham*

CONDIMENTS

SPICINESS RATING 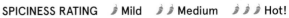 🌶 Mild 🌶🌶 Medium 🌶🌶🌶 Hot!

ORIGINS

Don Juan de Oñate brought green chilli seeds with him from Mexico in 1598 when he settled New Mexico as a Spanish colony, and chillies became part of the local diet. The recipe for modern-day green chile is probably a combination of Spanish and Native American cooking techniques, melding chopped roasted Hatch green chillies with onions, spices and chicken stock or water to make a thick, reduced sauce.

SERVES 6–8

NEW MEXICO, USA

GREEN CHILE

This thick, smoky, mouth-tingling sauce made from roasted green chillies, used as a condiment atop everything from burgers to burritos, is synonymous with the southwestern state of New Mexico.

YOU'LL NEED

1 small onion, peeled and chopped
1 tbs olive oil
1 clove of garlic, peeled and minced
1 tbs flour
½ cup (125mL) chicken or vegetable stock
300g (11oz) roast green chillies, peeled, seeded and chopped
1 large tomato, chopped
½ tsp cumin
½ tsp salt

METHOD

1 Saute onion in the oil over medium heat in a large saucepan for a few minutes.

2 Add the garlic and cook until the onion has softened.

3 Stir in the flour and cook for 2 minutes.

4 Slowly add the stock, stirring continuously.

5 Add the chillies, tomato, cumin and salt.

6 Cover the pan and simmer for 30 minutes, stirring occasionally. Leave to cool.

7 Serve immediately, or store, covered, in the refrigerator.

TASTING NOTES

In late summer, the crisp desert air of New Mexico takes on an exotic smoky scent as vendors set up shop in empty lots with sacks of green chillies and large metal tumble-roasters. Customers buy sacks of chillies, hand them to the roaster, and watch them spin over an open fire until their skins are ashy black. Try green chile at a dusty New Mexican roadhouse, where it oozes out from atop a juicy bison burger; order a green chile-smothered plate of French fries at a fast-food joint, trying hard not to drip on your shirt; or dine on grilled prawns with green chile at one of the après-ski restaurants in the arty resort towns of Santa Fe or Taos. ● by Emily Matchar

ORIGINS

The Spanish first introduced the red-hot harissa chilli peppers of the New World to Tunisia in the 1500s, bringing a little more heat to the country's cooking. The term 'harissa' derives from the Arabic 'to break into pieces', harking back to the crushing of desiccated chillies in a pestle and mortar that gave birth to this fiery condiment, and it was the Arabs who introduced the paste to Moroccan cuisine, finding the local dishes a little too bland.

SERVES 4

TUNISIA

HARISSA

Harissa, a thick flaming-red paste, oozes Mediterranean zest with a tantalising clash of bold tastes, uniting crushed garlic, dried chilli and sharp seasonings to embody the essence of Tunisian cuisine.

YOU'LL NEED

3 large dried red chillies, stems removed (double the chilli quantity to ramp up the spicy hit)
2 cloves of garlic, peeled and chopped
1 tsp ground coriander
1 tsp ground cumin
1 tsp caraway seeds
Salt (to taste)
Olive oil

METHOD

1 Roughly chop the chillies and soak them in boiling water for about an hour.

2 Drain and dry the chillies with a paper towel before placing them in a blender along with the garlic, coriander, cumin and caraway seeds.

3 Season with a little salt and a dash of olive oil, and blend together until the ingredients become a thick, smooth paste.

4 Spoon the mixture into a clean jar and cover with a 1cm (½ in) layer of olive oil. You can store it in the fridge for several weeks.

TIP *Harissa enlivens many Tunisian dishes, including breads, eggs, salads, pasta and couscous, and is said to aid digestion.*

TASTING NOTES

Feast your eyes on seductive mounds of harissa as you meander through a bustling fresh-produce souk (market), before stopping for lunch in the heaving heart of an ancient Tunisian medina. Begin with a simple serving of harissa topped with olive oil, inhaling the deceptively sweet chilli scent before plunging a slice of *tabouna* (Tunisian flat bread) into the mix; wait for the kick to come. Savour how garlic granules and chilli chunks fire up the smoky roasted peppers, tomatoes and smooth oils of a *salade mechouia*, or drizzle a little harissa over plain couscous and taste those traditionally tame grains spring to life as the spice sinks in. Wash away the burn local-style with *thé à la menthe* (mint tea). ● *by Isabella Noble*

ORIGINS

Ancient Greeks considered horseradish an aphrodisiac and painkiller. Legend has it that the Oracle of Delphi told Apollo it was worth its weight in gold. In the first millennium AD, the root spread to Central Europe and Scandinavia to be used as medicine and garnish. By the 1600s, it was an accompaniment to beef and oysters in Britain and by the 1850s, it had moved to America, where Central Europeans set up horseradish farms in the Midwest.

EUROPE & ASIA

HORSERADISH

Horseradish is spicy in a different way from chilli, but is just as intense. The gnarled beige root looks innocuous, but cut it open and the bitter pungency is eye-watering.

HORSERADISH & ROAST BEEF SANDWICH

YOU'LL NEED

2 thick slices brown bread
4 slices roast beef
Jarred horseradish (or make your own; see below)
Handful of rocket (arugula)

Horseradish
1 root of horseradish
2 tbs water
1 tbs white wine vinegar
3/5 cup (150mL) double cream
Salt

METHOD

1 Peel then roughly chop the horseradish root. Shred it through the grater in a food blender with a little water. Add the vinegar and then the double cream and seasoning to taste.

2 Spread prepared horseradish on bread to taste. Top with sliced roast beef and rocket, and finish it off by sandwiching the filling with the second slice of bread.

TASTING NOTES

A cruciferous root vegetable related to broccoli and cabbage, horseradish resembles a thick, creamy-tan carrot. Native to Europe and western Asia, it certainly gets around, appearing in different guises all over the world. Add zing to your English roast beef with a sauce of grated horseradish and vinegar, or use it to cut the fattiness of your Polish *kielbasa*. In Germany, take a bracing nip of horseradish schnapps, or wash down your horseradish-topped sausage with some horseradish beer. Add a counterpoint to sharp Wisconsin cheddar with a horseradish-and-cheese sandwich. Or, come brunch time, wake yourself up with a sinus-clearing horseradish-spiked Bloody Mary cocktail. Bottoms up! ● *by Emily Matchar*

YOU'LL NEED

1 large head of napa cabbage
  (Chinese cabbage)
½ cup coarse sea salt

Spicy sauce
½ cup coarse Korean red
  pepper powder
3 cloves of garlic, peeled and
  finely chopped
5cm (2in) piece of ginger
  root, peeled and finely
  chopped
½ medium pear, peeled and
  cored
1 tbs sesame seeds
¼ cup (60mL) *jeotgal* (fish
  juice)

ORIGINS

Kimchi dates back to antiquity
when vegetables were salted
to ensure a winter food supply.
Chilli peppers probably came to
Korea in the late 16th century
when Japan invaded the
country. Initially viewed with
scepticism and thought to be
poisonous, spicy vegetables
were commonplace by the
1800s, as was adding salted
seafood to kimchi. The final key
ingredient in today's kimchi,
napa cabbage, arrived in Korea
via China about 100 years ago.

SOUTH KOREA

KIMCHI

MAKES
ABOUT 8
CUPS

What happens when the world's favourite spicy fruit – the red chilli pepper – meets humdrum cabbage? Kimchi, that's what – the salty, spicy, fermented staple of this tiny Asian nation.

METHOD

1 Cut the cabbage lengthwise. Cut each piece again to make four quarters and discard the stem. Chop the cabbage into 1cm (2/5in) pieces.

2 Place the cabbage in a large stainless steel bowl, sprinkle on the salt and mix together with your hands. Let it sit 1–2 hours, or until the cabbage is slightly tender, but not wilted.

3 Wash and drain the cabbage three times, then place in a colander and drain for 1 hour.

4 Place the sauce ingredients in a blender. Blitz to a fine consistency then let it sit for at least 10 minutes.

5 Place the drained cabbage in a large

stainless steel bowl. Add the sauce and mix together with your hands (use plastic gloves to protect your hands).

6 Pack the cabbage into plastic containers (or mason jars) with tight-fitting lids. This is fresh kimchi and it's ready to eat.

7 For a deeper, more pungent flavour, let it stand at room temperature for 48 hours, then refrigerate. The longer it sits, the more pungent and sour the flavour and aroma.

TIP *This is a simplified recipe for fast kimchi. You'll get genuine kimchi with less fuss. All of the speciality ingredients can be purchased at a Korean grocer.*

TASTING NOTES

Kimchi is a gastronomic enigma wrapped in a leaf. First encounters are rarely enticing; the acrid aroma can knock back even the most adventurous foodie. Suppress that gag reflex and you'll be rewarded with crunchy leaves covered with a piquant mélange of hard-to-identify flavours that vary slightly with each bite. To experience kimchi's versatility, and Korea's lively dining culture, head to a barbecue-meat restaurant. Billowing smoke from charcoal briquettes, the crackle of sizzling pork and the din of *soju* (distilled alcohol)-inspired chatter all signal the beginning of an exceptional dinner. On your own tabletop BBQ, grill kimchi until golden. Use the tongs to place pork, garlic and roasted kimchi on a garden-fresh sesame leaf. Wrap it. Eat it. Relish it. ● *by Rob Whyte*

ORIGINS

Indian lime pickle is an attempt
to preserve summer. Limes are
harvested during the cool rainy
season, and 'pickled down' to
provide that vivid, citrus tang
all year round. The initial salting
takes two weeks, and you can
add another week for the pickle
to mature once cooked to bring
out the spicy goodness. Every
Indian family has a carefully
guarded recipe, but pickling
is a tradition that dates back
to at least Vedic times
(1700 BC–150 BC).

MAKES
500ML

INDIA, PAKISTAN & BANGLADESH

LIME PICKLE

Across the Indian subcontinent, *nimbu* or *naranga achar* –
made with salt, mustard oil, ground chilli and spices – is
not just a condiment, it's the cornerstone of every meal.

YOU'LL NEED

12 limes, cut into eight
  segments, then in half again
½ cup of salt (ideally a mix
  of white sea salt and black
  rock salt)
6 tsp mustard seeds, ground
6 tsp fennel seeds, dry-
  roasted then ground
6 tbs ground dried chilli
2 tsp turmeric powder
2 cups (500mL) mustard oil
2 tsp whole mustard seeds
1 tsp asafoetida

METHOD

1 Take a sterilised pickling jar and add the chopped limes and
salt, then mix together and seal the jar. Keep in a light place
for two weeks for the salt to do its work.

2 Add the ground mustard and fennel seeds, chilli and the
turmeric.

3 Next, heat the mustard oil to smoking point, add the mustard
seeds and the asafoetida, then turn off the heat. Pour the hot
mixture over the limes.

4 Allow the pickle to cool, then leave it to mature for at least
a week before serving.

TASTING NOTES

Forget everything you know about Indian pickles from eating poppadoms in Indian
restaurants overseas. Mango chutney is just glorified jam; the real deal is lime pickle
– the oily red condiment that appears on the side of almost every plate served in the
subcontinent. This is not just a dip – locals will eat it with *papad* (the real Indian poppadom),
with rice, with vegetables, with curry, with just about anything. But be warned, it packs
a punch. The combination of hot chilli, salt and tart lime is vibrant and immediate, like a
defibrillator applied to the taste buds. It sometimes contains large chunks of lime – it's wise
to chop these into smaller morsels or the flavours can be overwhelming. ● *by Joe Bindloss*

ORIGINS

Aleppo in northern Syria has been a bubbling cauldron of culinary influences through the centuries. Hot-yet-sweet Aleppo pepper has been a favoured spice of the city's chefs since ancient times. *Muhummara* is widely acknowledged to have first been made within the city walls; the recipe then passed down by memory from cook to cook, spreading all across the Middle Eastern region, long before written recipes became commonplace.

MUHUMMARA

SERVES 4

This fiery pesto-like spiced walnut paste will set your taste buds tingling. Putting some serious heat into Middle Eastern meze, *muhummara* is the dip you aren't likely to forget.

YOU'LL NEED

3 red capsicums
¾ cup fresh, toasted breadcrumbs
¾ cup ground walnuts
2 cloves of garlic, peeled and minced
2 tbs Aleppo pepper flakes (available at Middle Eastern and Turkish speciality stores and sometimes called *pul biber*)
3 tbs lemon juice
3 tbs pomegranate molasses (available at Middle Eastern and Turkish speciality stores)
2 tbs olive oil
1 tsp cumin
Extra virgin olive oil for drizzling

METHOD

1 Preheat the oven to 200°C (400°F).

2 Roast the capsicums on a tray in the top of the oven, turning occasionally, until the skin is blackened and blistered (approximately 40 minutes).

3 Remove from the oven, seal in a plastic bag and allow to cool.

4 Peel and seed the capsicums and place into a food processor along with the remaining ingredients. Blend the mixture to a paste.

5 Serve in a central bowl and finish with a drizzle of extra virgin olive oil.

TASTING NOTES

A meze spread is Middle Eastern food at its most flavoursome, with the morsels of intermingling tastes shared and lingered over. The flashy bowl of potent-red *muhummara* makes its entrance beside the blander shades of dipping staples hummus and baba ganoush. With torn bread, scoop the *muhummara* straight from the bowl – the first taste is all sharp heat from the fresh or roasted red capsicum and the dried Aleppo pepper flakes (known as *pul biber* in Turkey), but the sting is tempered by the paste's subtle fruity sour undertones from the pomegranate molasses and lemon juice. To complete the experience, make like a local and order a milky arak to see how this aniseed-flavoured liqueur complements *muhummara's* intense bite. ● *by Jess Lee*

ORIGINS

Northern-hemispherians have used mustard for 2000 years – adding a palate-punch before Eastern spices arrived. The Romans made it a condiment, grinding seeds with young wine ('*must*') took it to France and, in 1777 created mild Dijon mustard. Jeremiah Colman, a miller from Norwich, restored mustard's fire – in 1814 he devised a way to powder the seeds without evaporating their heat-giving oils. He was appointed mustard-maker to Queen Victoria.

MAKES
600ML

ENGLAND

MUSTARD

**Medicine to the Greeks, a spread to the Romans, beloved
by Gallic monks – mustard's been popular for millennia,
across continents. But it's in England that it's at its fiery best.**

YOU'LL NEED

125g (4½oz) brown mustard
   seeds
30g (1oz) yellow mustard
   seeds
1 cup (275mL) white-wine
   vinegar
1 cup (250mL) beer
125g (4½oz) mustard powder
1 cup (250mL) cold water
1 tsp sugar
1 tsp salt

METHOD

1 Combine the mustard seeds, vinegar and beer in a bowl.
Cover and leave for 48 hours. It does not need to be
refrigerated.

2 Transfer the mix to a food processor; add the remaining
ingredients.

3 Process until smooth (about 5 minutes).

4 Decant into a glass jar; seal and refrigerate.

5 Allow the flavours to develop for 3-4 weeks.

TIP *You can buy it in a jar, but making your own mustard
means you can control its kick. Plus, mix in a few extras to
give your mustard extra punch – the addition of beer seems
especially England-appropriate...*

TASTING NOTES

English mustard has a colour akin to the contents of a newborn's nappy. But get over that,
this stuff is a taste sensation. Picture the scene: you've rocked up for lunch at a traditional
boozer – one that hasn't gone gastro – and a limp ham sandwich has appeared. Your
stomach starts to sink, but then... stuffed amid the sticky sachets you spot it: Colman's
English Mustard. A quick squeeze and your snack's transformed. Your nose starts to burn,
your eyes to glisten, your taste buds declare 'thank you!' Mustard is the soul-mate of quality
produce and the elevator of the mediocre. For the most satisfying combo, eat it with pork
pies or cold cuts. Just remember, it's hot! ● *by Sarah Baxter*

ORIGINS

Said to be the most ancient among Thai dishes, this paste was, and still is, made with the pestle and mortar. Early versions mixed peppercorns with fermented soy beans and charred shallots, providing heat and salt, alongside a souring agent, such as lime juice or fresh tamarind. As the Thais moved south, they discovered and added coconuts, palm sugar and fermented fish. And as chillies arrived in the 16th century, they too were thrown in.

TASTING NOTES

The classic *nam phrik gapi* is both pungent and delicate, a wonderful mix of raw garlic, shrimp paste, palm sugar, fish sauce, lime juice... and a mind-blowing quantity of bird's-eye chillies. The first taste is deep, before the tiny fruits kick in and get the heart beating faster. But as in all Thai food, balance – between the salty, sweet, sour and hot – is everything. A bitter version is made with pea eggplants, while in the south it's made with coconut. Some have pork as a main ingredient, others green pepper, tamarind, minced prawns and salted duck egg. But remember... *nam phrik* is never, ever eaten alone. ● *by Tom Parker Bowles*

SERVES 8

THAILAND

NAM PHRIK

In Thailand, you're never more than a few feet from *nam phrik*, a pungent, spicy shrimp-and-chilli relish that's eaten alongside everything from omelettes to fish cakes, deep-fried prawns and pork.

NAM PHRIK GUNG

YOU'LL NEED
4 cloves of garlic, peeled
Pinch of salt
2 coriander roots
4 shallots, grilled or roasted
8 bird's eye chillies
½ tsp shrimp paste
Some chicken stock
1–2 tbs palm sugar
½ tbs lime juice
Dash of fish sauce
2 tbs pea eggplants
Handful of small prawns

METHOD
1 Grind the garlic, salt and coriander roots into a paste with a mortar and pestle.

2 Peel the grilled (or roasted) shallots and add them, with the chillies and shrimp paste. Pound the mixture, adding stock to keep it moist.

3 Mix in the palm sugar, lime juice and fish sauce to taste.

4 Finally, add the pea eggplants and prawns and crush with the pestle so both are bruised. This coarse, hot, salty condiment can be served with meat or raw/blanched vegetables.

TIP *There are dozens of varieties of nam phrik in Thailand. This one, adapted from the master Thai chef David Thompson, of Nahm restaurant in Bangkok, features pea eggplants and prawns.*

YOU'LL NEED

2 red capsicums, seeded and
  finely chopped
2 green capsicums, seeded
  and finely chopped
10 jalapeño chillies, seeded
  and finely chopped
1 cup (250mL) cider vinegar
1 packet (6g) fruit pectin
1kg (2lb) sugar

ORIGINS

Though the exact origins of
pepper jelly are unclear, it is
presumed to have been invented
by early settlers to Southern USA
to preserve the chillies that grew
there. Different regions have
different styles – Texas pepper
jelly usually contains jalapeños,
for example, while St Augustine
in North Florida uses unique
datil chillies brought by Chilean
immigrants. Most use sweet red
bell peppers (capsicums) as the
base, though green pepper jelly
is not uncommon.

SOUTHERN USA

PEPPER JELLY

As rosy orange as sunset in a jar, sweet-spicy pepper jelly on a tray with crackers and cream cheese is a quintessential part of any proper Southern dinner party.

METHOD

1 Place the capsicum and chillies in a large saucepan and add the vinegar.

2 Stir in the pectin.

3 Bring the mixture to the boil over a high heat.

4 Stir in the sugar and return to the boil for 1 minute, stirring constantly.

5 Remove from the heat and skim away any foam with a slotted spoon.

6 Ladle into pre-sterilised glass jars or other heatproof containers.

7 The jelly will last for 2–3 weeks if stored in the refrigerator.

TASTING NOTES

The classic way to taste red pepper jelly is as an appetiser, served with crackers and cream cheese. The sweet heat of the jelly is a perfect contrast to the cool, unctuous cheese. Subbing goat's cheese for cream cheese is a slightly more sophisticated take on the concept, bringing an element of tanginess to the party. Pepper jelly also makes an excellent glaze for meats, turning ham, chicken wings or shrimp into instant sweet-spicy delights. The bold may even enjoy slightly softened pepper jelly over vanilla ice cream, the potent, vinegary kick of the jelly cutting through the richness of the ice cream. ● *by Emily Matchar*

YOU'LL NEED

500g (1lb) cauliflower florets
2 onions, peeled and
  chopped
100g (3½oz) French beans
Salt for brining
2¾ cups (700mL) malt vinegar
2 tbs coriander seeds
Pinch salt
3 tbs English mustard powder
3 tbs plain flour
1 tbs ground turmeric
2 tsp ground ginger
¼ cup (50mL) cider vinegar
2 cloves of garlic, peeled and
  crushed
200g (7oz) granulated sugar

ORIGINS

Even the Oxford English
Dictionary can't fathom where
the word 'piccalilli' comes
from, classing it as of 'uncertain
origin'. The spelling has varied
too: peccalillo, pickalilly,
pickylilly... It was also once
called Indian pickle, which nods
to its roots – it seems to be
an Anglicisation of India *achar*
(pickles), mixing the new spices
arriving from the Empire with
English ingredients. The first
known recipe was printed in *Art
of Cookery* in 1758.

DORLING KINDERSLEY © GETTY IMAGES, ANDERS, BEN/THE FOOD PASSIONATES © CORBIS

ENGLAND

PICCALILLI

MAKES
3 TO 4 JARS

This 'Indian pickle' is like edible potpourri, a chutney-ish jumble of chopped vegetables and spices, pickled in vinegar. Not much to look, but a tasty addition to many a meal.

METHOD

1 Put the vegetables in a large bowl, sprinkle over a layer of salt, mix well, cover and leave for 24 hours.

2 Rinse the vegetables well with cold water, then pat dry with a dish towel.

3 Put the vinegar, coriander seeds and salt in a large pan and bring to the boil. Add the cauliflower and onion; simmer until slightly softened.

4 Meanwhile, put the mustard powder, flour, turmeric and ginger in a bowl; whisk in the cider vinegar until smooth, then set aside.

5 Add the beans, garlic and sugar to the pan; stir until the sugar has dissolved then drain over a bowl to collect the vinegar.

6 Put the mustard mix and vinegar back into the pan. Bring to the boil, then simmer for 10 minutes.

7 Return the drained vegetables to the pan. Add more sugar and water if necessary to give a thick consistency, then take the pan off the heat.

8 Decant into sterilised, sealable jars. Store for 3 months in cool, dark place before eating.

TIP *You can chuck in any vegetables you want – use what's seasonal, and what you like – just make sure they are all even bite-sized pieces.*

TASTING NOTES

Fêtes, fairs, country-shows – piccalilli is a stalwart at these traditional affairs – and a jar of this garish relish might be found loitering at the back of many an English cupboard or fridge – possibly untouched. It's a bit of a Marmite: most either love or hate its curious, vaguely curried crunch of seasonal veg, which may include cauliflower, beans, onions and small cucumbers. But order a ploughman's lunch and take the plunge – a platter of English cheese, crusty bread, crisp celery, and perhaps a slab of ham, are the perfect canvas for a daub of piccalilli. Its mild yet discernible turmeric and mustard tang enhances the flavours – not to mention adding a splash of colour, too. ● *by Sarah Baxter*

ORIGINS

Although the origins of *pol sambola* aren't known, it's not surprising that Sri Lankan cooks combined two easily sourced ingredients – coconut and chilli – to make what is today one of the nation's most popular condiments. Coconuts have been a staple crop for the island since at least the Rohana Kingdom (210–161 BC), but chillies were only introduced by colonial-era trading ships in the 17th century, so the dish must have evolved after then.

SERVES 2

SRI LANKA

POL SAMBOLA

This coconut-rich spicy *sambol* (chutney) sums up tropical
Sri Lanka. Its tingling heat, tempered by candy-sugar coconut,
is sunshine and lazy beach days for your taste buds.

YOU'LL NEED
½ red onion, peeled and
  finely diced
3 dried red chillies
1 tsp chilli powder
1 tbs Maldive fish (optional)
Juice of 1 lime
3 cups grated flesh of fresh
  coconut
Salt to taste

METHOD
1 Using a mortar and pestle (or a food processor) grind up the
red onion, dried red chillies, chilli powder, Maldive fish and half
of the lime juice until it becomes a paste.

2 Add the coconut and the rest of the lime juice and combine
by hand until the mixture is an even orange-red colour. Add
salt to taste.

TASTING NOTES
A sticky-looking orange side dish appears without fanfare on your table. Under the rhythmic
thwack-thwack of the restaurant's wobbling ceiling fans, the Sri Lankans at the table next
to yours are spooning generous dollops of this stuff on to their rice. Do as they do to
discover why the *pol sambola* bowl is often the first one emptied. The initial taste is the
fruity sweetness of coconut, but a punch of chilli soon makes its presence known. There's
sourness as well, thanks to a generous dousing of lime and, if the cook has used Maldive
fish, a salty note adds a final bite. Sweet, salty, sour and spicy, *pol sambola* is the piquant
antidote to a humid Sri Lankan day. ● *by Jess Lee*

ORIGINS

Xnipec has been prepared in the Yucatán peninsula for over 8000 years, since the first habañero peppers were grown domestically. Habañeros come from the Amazonia region in South America and it is believed they reached Mexico via Cuba (hence the name habañero for Habana, the capital). Their scientific name, however, is *Capsicum chinense* thanks to a Dutch botanist named Nikolaus J von Jacquin, who mistakenly believed they originated in China.

SERVES 4

THE YUCATÁN PENINSULA, MEXICO

SALSA XNIPEC

Xnipec means 'the dog's nose' in Mayan so prepare for
some nose-tingling snuffles after tasting this fiery salsa made
from blazing-hot habañeros blitzed with sour citrus juice!

YOU'LL NEED

4–5 habañero peppers
⅔ cup (170mL) sour orange
    juice or use a combination
    of lime juice, lime zest and
    grapefruit juice
¼ cup fresh coriander leaves
    (cilantro), chopped
Salt to taste

TIP *Use this spicy table condiment over scrambled eggs,
grilled meats, rice and beans,
and, why not, a good slice
of pizza.*

METHOD

1 Over an open flame on the stove or a barbecue, roast the
habañeros until the skin blackens. In Yucatán cooks often
roast the habañeros by placing them directly over hot
charcoal coals.

2 Using a pestle and mortar, crush the habañeros, adding
enough juice to make a salsa. Add the coriander and salt
to taste.

3 Adjust the seasoning and let it rest for half an hour or so.

TASTING NOTES

Xnipec goes best with food from the Yucatán region. At the Lucas de Vargas Market in
Mérida, people sprinkle *xnipec* over freshly made *panuchos* (black-bean-stuffed tortillas
topped with chicken or turkey), and tacos with *cochinita pibil* (slow-roasted, marinated
pork, sour oranges and annatto seeds wrapped in banana leaves). Although the kick can
be extreme, it is tamed with pickled red onions, which provide a cool contrast. Luckily, you
don't have to travel far to get a *xnipec* hit – if you can find habañeros then you can easily
make your own. But beware, *xnipec* is not for the faint of heart and if you go too far you may
find your nose getting as wet as your dog's! ● *By Mauricio Velázquez de León*

ORIGINS

Sambal was originally an Indonesian word, but today the term is used across the region, and even as far afield as Sri Lanka and the Philippines. Now integral to Indonesian cooking, the condiment owes its existence to the spice trade from South America to Spain and Portugal and on to Spanish and Portuguese colonies in Southeast Asia. This was how the chilli first arrived in Asia, and Asian cooking was never the same again.

MALAYSIA & INDONESIA

SAMBAL ULEK

No, that innocent blob of red sauce isn't ketchup, it's *sambal ulek* – Indonesian chilli paste, a fiery mix of raw red chillies and *terasi* (*belacan*) – toasted shrimp paste.

YOU'LL NEED

4 tbs vegetable oil
20 fresh red chillies, sliced
10 shallots, peeled and chopped
4 cloves of garlic, peeled and chopped
1 fresh tomato, chopped
1 tsp toasted shrimp paste (*terasi/belacan*)
1 tsp salt
1½ tsp palm sugar

METHOD

1 Heat oil in a wok and add the chilli, shallots and garlic. Fry until the chillies and shallots are soft.

2 Add the tomato and continue to fry for another minute, then transfer the mixture to a pestle and mortar.

3 Crush and grind the ingredients together with the toasted shrimp paste, salt and palm sugar, and work the mixture into a coarse paste.

4 Transfer to a jar and keep in the fridge until needed.

TASTING NOTES

Taste it tentatively, is our advice. You may find a dollop of this culinary napalm on the side of your plate, or in a bowl or dish on your table. Do not be lulled into false sense of security. This is not the local ketchup, this is preserved fire. As you deposit the first morsel into your mouth, you can expect a hammer-blow hit of chilli, and the heat will be even more ferocious if the sambal is freshly prepared. Then you'll notice the other flavours: the salt and sugar, the garlic, and the fishy tone added by the *terasi* (*belacan*). The trick is to take small blobs with each forkful; stirring a spoonful into your meal is unwise... ● *By Joe Bindloss*

ORIGINS

It is believed that wasabi was originally used for medicinal purposes in medieval Japan and it was not until the Edo period that its popularity as a condiment and ingredient in Japanese cookery grew due to its formal cultivation. In addition to its flavour and ability to disguise the strong smell of the sea, it is likely that wasabi's anti-bacterial and deodorising properties led to its use with raw fish.

YOU'LL NEED

1 part freshly grated or pre-prepared wasabi
10 parts whole-egg mayonnaise
300g (11oz) sashimi-grade salmon, chopped in small cubes
1 medium avocado, diced
1 shallot, peeled and finely diced
Juice of 1 lime
Handful of dill
Salt and pepper
Salad leaves to serve

JAPAN

WASABI

One of Japanese cuisine's magical ingredients, indigenous wasabi –
a knobbly, pale-green root vegetable with bright-green flesh – has
a pungent yet refreshing taste that elevates sashimi to dizzying heights.

SALMON TARTARE WITH
WASABI MAYONNAISE

METHOD

1 To make the wasabi mayonnaise, mix the
freshly grated wasabi with the mayonnaise.

2 For the salmon tartare, mix the wasabi
mayonnaise with the salmon, avocado, shallot,
lime juice and dill.

3 Pack the salmon mixture into a round cookie
cutter or mould on a plate.

4 Carefully lift the cutter or mould, season
the salmon mixture with salt and pepper and
garnish with salad leaves to serve.

TIP *Use wasabi paste if you can't find fresh
wasabi. This mayonnaise can also be used as a
dipping sauce for grilled meats and vegetables.*

TASTING NOTES

Wasabi thrives in Japan's cold, pure running water, which is why it is difficult to source
outside Japan. Those used to the ubiquitous sachets or the powdered pastes served in sushi
restaurants might be surprised to learn that their hotness is due to the harsher horseradish,
which is often used to supplement the more-expensive wasabi. Fresh wasabi root on its
own is rather bitter but, freshly grated, it's a revelation – more delicate and fragrant than
horseradish, the initial pungent 'hit' lasts only a few seconds after grating and delivers a
refreshing taste. Fresh wasabi is best eaten on its own, not mixed with soy sauce, on sushi
or sashimi or as a palate-cleanser between different raw-fish dishes. ● *By Johanna Ashby*

GLOSSARY

acuka Turkish name for muhammara.

ají amarillo A Peruvian yellow chilli pepper, turning orange as it matures.

ají limo A Peruvian chilli with a spicy, yet distinctive citrus flavour when cooked. It's commonly used in ceviche, salsa and rice dishes.

Aleppo pepper Commonly used in Middle Eastern/Mediterranean cuisine, it has a moderate heat with a bit of a cumin, fruity undertone.

allspice Not to be confused with mixed spice or five-spice, allspice is a key ingredient in Caribbean jerk seasoning and made with the dried, unripe berries of a pimento tree.

amchur Ground mango powder used in Indian cooking.

annatto paste/seed Used in Mexican and Caribbean cooking to give a rich, saffron-like colour. Try a blend of turmeric and paprika as a substitute.

añejo A sharp Mexican cheese made from either goats' or cows' milk, flavoured with paprika. Good for grilling or baking. Parmesan or feta can be used as a substitute.

árbol see **chile de árbol**.

atchar Spicy pickles – a South African condiment usually made with unripe green mangoes and chillies and served with curry.

baharat An Arabian spice blend consisting of allspice, cardamom seeds, cassia bark, cloves, coriander seeds, nutmeg, dried red chilli/paprika and peppercorns.

belacan Malay shrimp paste. Used widely in Asian countries and purchased in blocks.

berbere A spice mixture from Ethiopia and Eretria, featuring the rare Ajwain seed, along with chilli, garlic, ginger, dried basil, cloves, fenugreek, cardamom and coriander and other ingredients.

bird's-eye chilli A small chilli found in Southeast Asia, technically medium in heat, but more than hot enough for most people.

candlenuts An Indonesian staple used to thicken spice pastes. Macadamia nuts would be the best choice for a substitute.

cassareep A key ingredient in Guyanese pepperpot; a thick black liquid made from cassava.

cassava A tuberous root and major source of carbohydrate in the developing world. Has a delicate flavour and accompanies meat. Boiled or fried potatoes could be a fair substitute.

cayenne pepper Hot and pungent, used powdered, whole, in dried flakes or in a vinegar-based sauce. Red chilli powder or paprika can be substitutes.

ceviche A dish of fresh, raw fish marinated in citrus juice (lemons or limes) until 'cooked' by the acid. Unlike escabeche, ceviche is not cooked prior to marinading, so the freshness of the fish is paramount.

chile de árbol A small Mexican chilli pepper also known as bird's-beak chilli/rat's-tail chilli. Can be substituted with cayenne pepper.

Chinese five-spice A classic mixture of spices used in Chinese cooking, ingredients usually comprise star anise, cloves, fennel seeds, Sichuan pepper and Chinese cinnamon.

Chinese cinnamon Also known as cassia cinnamon. Has a more pungent, stronger taste than Ceylon (real) cinnamon, as Chinese cinnamon contains 5% cassia to Ceylon's milder 0.4%.

chipotle A smoke-dried jalapeño chilli – used primarily in Mexican cooking, with a mild, earthy spiciness. Ideal in salsas, for meat marinades or added whole to soups and stews.

çiğ köfte Translates as 'raw meatballs' in Turkish, it is the finest lean raw beef (or lamb), ground with onions, tomato paste and bulgur (cracked wheat), laced with isot pepper.

cloves A very strong spice, native to Indonesia. Commonly available, but try a mixture of allspice, cinnamon and nutmeg if a substitute is required.

cumin An aromatic spice available whole (as a dried seed) or ground; used to flavour curries and soups. Use caraway seeds (half as much) as a substitute.

doro wat An Ethiopian stew or curry, traditionally prepared with chicken, egg and onion laced with berbere spice mixture.

epazote A herb with a strong, acidic taste used to flavour Mexican dishes. Can be difficult to source/substitute – try combining cumin, oregano and coriander.

escabeche Poached/fried fish marinated in an acidic mixture, served cold and name of the marinade itself. See also ceviche.

fenugreek Available in seed or dried herb format, or as a fresh vegetable. The yellow seeds are a popular feature of Ethiopian and Indian cooking, particularly in dhals and spice mixes.

fufu A staple in West African cooking – yams or cassava pounded into a dough. Pinch off a bit of fufu with your right hand and dip into soups.

galangal A rhizome, similar in appearance to ginger, purchase fresh (use a sharp knife to slice) or powdered. Ginger can be used in its place, but it is much milder than galangal.

garam masala A sweet blend of spices including cardamom, cumin, pepper and star anise.

ghee Clarified butter.

ginger flower Also known as torch ginger. In Southeast Asia the bud of this beautiful flower is used to make laksa. Can be purchased frozen from large Asian grocery stores.

gochujang A savoury Korean condiment of red pepper paste, comprising red chilli, rice, fermented soybeans and salt.

guajillo chilli A reddish-brown Mexican chilli pepper. Moderately hot in flavour. Used in salsas, pastes and meat rubs.

guaque chilli A Guatemalan chilli pepper.

gula melaka The Indonesian name for palm sugar.

habanero chilli An intensely hot chilli pepper that can vary in colour (unripe are green, other colours include orange, red, white, brown and pink).

hae ko Prawn paste – a common ingredient in Asian cuisine.

harissa A hot chilli sauce from Tunisia.

hawaji A Yemeni spice mix incorporating peppercorns, caraway seeds, saffron, cardamom and turmeric.

huajiao See **Sichuan pepper**.

huoguo Translates as 'fire pot' in Chinese – a simmering broth of chillies and Sichuan peppercorns in which various meat, seafood and vegetables are cooked, 'asian-fondue' style.

ika mata A raw fish salad with coconut, originating in Rarotonga (Cook Islands).

injera An Ethiopian fermented pancake with a spongy texture, traditionally eaten with wat or doro wat.

isot pepper A dried Turkish chilli pepper with a smoky, sultry taste. Used in meat and savoury foods with an initially mild heat that builds deceptively over time.

jalapeño pepper A medium-sized chilli pepper, usually picked when green.

jjigae A Korean dish similar to a stew, typically served in a communal dish with meat and vegetables.

Kampot pepper Available as green, black, red or white peppercorns, originating from the southern province of Kampot in Cambodia.

kecap manis Indonesian sweet soy sauce, extra syrupy when added to palm sugar. Regular soy sauce mixed with honey or molasses can be used instead.

kerisik A dense paste used in Malaysian and Indonesian cuisine – made from coconut roasted in a dry pan and ground in a mortar and pestle.

kimchi A Korean side dish of vegetables with a variety of seasonings. Has a spicy/sour flavour.

kitfo An Ethiopian dish consisting of raw minced beef that has been blended with a chilli-based spice mix and doused in melted, clarified butter.

kombu Edible kelp. Kombu is the only seaweed that can be used to make stock.

la douban jiang A hot paste of red chilli peppers, fermented broad beans, soy beans, salt, rice and spices, popular in Sichuan cuisine.

lajiaojiang Chinese hot chilli paste.

laksa leaves A weirdly metallic tasting mint, with strong pepper notes. Use mint and coriander as a substitute. Also known as Vietnamese mint.

leaf masala A blend of cumin, coriander, fennel, paprika and bay leaves. Ideal for curries.

lemongrass A popular herb in Asian cuisine and can be purchased whole, dried or powdered. As the name suggests, it has a citrus flavour.

lontong Compressed rice cake, usually served cold or room temperature with Indonesian dishes.

machaca A Mexican dish of dried, spiced and shredded beef or pork jerky, usually served with flour tortillas.

ma-la Meaning numbing and spicy – the repercussions of eating ma-la sauce; the numbness created by Sichuan peppercorns.

mirchi ka pakoda An Indian snack of whole chillies in batter.

mirin A sweet rice wine used commonly in Japanese cooking. Although similar to sake, mirin is lower in alcohol and has a higher sugar content, which adds a mild sweetness to dishes and sauces.

mole A slow-cooked savoury Mexican sauce featuring chilli peppers, herbs, spices and occasionally dark chocolate.

muhummara A Syrian dip, using fresh or roasted red capsicum pounded with ground walnuts, olive oil and breadcrumbs, with dried Aleppo pepper, pomegranate molasses, cumin, salt, garlic and lemon juice.

'nduja A Calabrian spicy, spreadable salami. Substitute with chorizo or any spicy Italian sausage.

nit'r qibe An Ethiopian spiced butter consisting of unsalted butter, black cardamom seeds, fenugreek powder and ground nigella seeds.

nori Edible seaweed commonly used as a wrap for sushi, but also as a garnish or flavouring in noodles and soups.

okra Five-sided small pods with an zucchini/eggplant taste. Used to thicken soups and stews due to the release of gelatinous substance when cooked.

omo tuo A Ghanese dish consisting of balls of sticky pudding rice – often accompanies soups.

otak-otak A Southeast Asian cake made with spiced fish paste, wrapped in a banana leaf and grilled over a charcoal fire. Also sold frozen or in canned varieties in Asian stores.

Padrón peppers (pimentos de Padrón) Small Spanish peppers – considered the Russian Roulette of peppers; while often mild, some can be really hot!

pandan leaves Long green leaves used in Southeast Asian cuisine for their sweet, toasted coconut/pecan/basmati flavour.

pepperoncino An Italian mild chilli, slightly bitter.

petai Known as the 'stink bean', not because of the odour, but you will after consuming it. Used in Southeast Asian cooking with other strongly flavoured foods.

pico de gallo Mexican salsa made from uncooked chopped tomato, white onion and chillis.

pul biber see **Aleppo pepper**.

queso fresco A Mexican fresh cheese, either made from raw cow's milk or a combination of cow and goat milk. Use feta or goat's cheese as a substitute.

ras el hanout A complex Moroccan spice blend (can feature up to 50 spices) commonly used in tagines and meat rubs.

sambal A particularly fiery salsa-like condiment featuring tomato, onion, carrot and chilli. Buy ready-made sambals at food markets or Asian grocery stores.

Scotch bonnet pepper A variety of chilli pepper found mostly in the Caribbean islands – popular in hot sauces and condiments. Also has some sweet varieties.

serrano pepper A popular chilli pepper used in Mexican cuisine.

Similar in appearance to a jalapeño chilli pepper but spicier.

Sichuan pepper A popular Asian spice. Can be used whole or, commonly, the powder features in Chinese five-spice. Sichuan pepper is not as hot as chilli pepper but has slightly zesty, lemony overtones.

star anise A star-shaped spice closely resembling liquorice in flavour, it's a traditional component of Chinese five-spice and garam masala. Substitute with anise seed, allspice or fennel seeds.

suanmiao A Chinese vegetable also known as garlic leeks. Use baby leeks or spring onions as a substitute.

sumac A citrus-tinged spice used in Middle Eastern cuisine.

Szechuan pepper see Sichuan pepper.

tai plaa A very hot Thai paste made with fermented fish innards.

tamarind juice Made from the mashed, ripened pulp of the tamarind pod. A base of Southeast Asian dishes, it is distinctively sweet and sour. Can be bought in Asian markets or use lemon or lime.

teff An Ethiopian grain used to make injera, high in iron, protein and calcium, similar in texture to quinoa or millet, but with a smaller seed that cooks faster.

tinga poblana A classic stew from the Puebla region of Mexico: shredded pork shoulder cooked with chipotle chillies.

tomatillo A light-green-husked Mexican fruit and a key ingredient in thickening sauces. Use green salsa or underripe tomatoes with lime juice as a substitute.

torch ginger see **ginger flower**.

turmeric This is a rhizome, like ginger but usually smaller. Beneath the dull orange peel, you'll find brilliant gold. Available fresh in Asian grocery stores, and as a ground spice almost everywhere.

Urfa biber see **isot pepper.**

Vietnamese mint A metallic-tasting mint, with strong pepper notes. Use mint and coriander as a substitute.

water spinach A popular vegetable for stir-fries in Southeast Asian countries. Look for it in Asian markets or substitute with watercress, snow pea leaves or spinach.

zaatar/zahtar The name of a Middle Eastern mixed herb and also a spice mixture, generally made from ground thyme, oregano and marjoram combined with toasted sesame seeds, sumac and salt.

AUTHORS

TOM PARKER BOWLES is a food writer with an ever-expanding gut. He has a weekly column in the *Mail on Sunday*, as well as being Food Editor of *Esquire*. He is also a Contributing Editor to *Departures* magazine. His first book, *E is for Eating: An Alphabet of Greed* (2004) was an opinionated romp through the world of food. His next, *The Year of Eating Dangerously* (2006) explored the more weird and exotic delicacies of the world. And his third, *Full English: A Journey Through the British and Their Food* was published in 2009 and won the Guild of Food Writers 2010 award for best work on British food. *Let's Eat* (2012) is a collection of his favourite recipes, gathered from around the world and recreated in his own kitchen. *Let's Eat Meat* (2014) is filled with recipes for meat. But is all about eating less meat, but better quality.

Tom is also a judge of *The Hotplate* on Australia's Channel 9. To counteract all that eating, he once joined a gym, but sadly, it disagreed with his delicate constitution.

Abigail Blasi Specialises in writing on Italy, and is dedicated to sampling the country's dazzling gastronomy and hunting down its spiciest flavours.

Adam Karlin Has covered India, Southeast Asia, Jamaica and the American South for Lonely Planet, so it's safe to say he's got a thing for bright, fiery foods.

Amy Karafin Lonely Planet *India* co-author and master scout of dirt-cheap vegetarian food the world over.

Anthony Ham Writer and photographer with a passion for food from Africa to the Arctic and from Spain to Syria.

Austin Bush Lonely Planet writer, writer/photographer behind the Thai food blog www. austinbushphotography.com, and contributor to publications including *Bon Appétit*, *Condé Nast Traveler*, *Lucky Peach*, *The New York Times* and *Saveur*.

Brett Atkinson Frequent traveller to Australia, Turkey and Southeast Asia, restaurant reviewer for viewauckland.co.nz, and incorrigible street food and craft beer fan.

Caroline Veldhuis Contributor to Lonely Planet travel/culture books, lifelong vegetarian and international culinary student who has been declared a 'messy' cook in both Vietnam and Turkey.

Emily Matchar Culture writer for magazines and newspapers; has contributed to more than a dozen Lonely Planet titles. Nashville-style chicken would be her jailhouse last meal.

Ethan Gelber Founder/editor of TheTravelWord.com; AFAR Ambassador; agitator for responsible and local travel; voracious consumer of culture, especially the edible kind.

Isabella Noble London-based lifelong vegetarian, with a fervent fear of tomatoes and an insatiable hunger for exploring the world, one beach at a time.

Joe Bindloss Former food critic for *Time Out*, specialising in food from Southeast Asia, China, Korea and the Indian subcontinent, and current Lonely Planet Destination Editor.

Jess Lee Co-author of Lonely Planet's *Turkey* and *Egypt*, Middle Eastern food-nut, once challenged a Turkish waiter to a hot pepper eating competition and won.

Johanna Ashby Food and travel freelance writer and specialist author for Lonely Planet, keen on street food to fine dining and everything in between.

Joshua Samuel Brown Purveyor of good eats from Singapore's hawker centres to Taiwan's night markets to Portland's food-truck scene, Joshua is co-author of a dozen-plus Lonely Planet guides.

Karyn Noble A London-based editor, writer and shameless epicurean. Australian by birth, she will happily debate the merits of Vegemite as a condiment.

Kate Thomas Lonely Planet West Africa author with a magic compass for tracking down fresh and fiery dishes from Liberia to Mali – and a firm belief that nothing beats the oysters in Guinea-Bissau.

Kate Whitfield Freelance writer, contributor to the since-departed Wine X magazine and Black Book restaurant guide, voracious traveller.

Lucy Corne Blogger on all things beer-related, co-author of Lonely Planet's *South Africa*, Lesotho & Swaziland, cake devourer and offal avoider.

Luke Waterson Co-author of Lonely Planet's Mexico, Peru and Cuba, contributor to The World's Best Street Food, Food/Travel writer for the BBC. Addicted to Oaxaca's chillies.

Mark Beales Co-author of Lonely Planet Thailand, dedicated

foodie and curry connoisseur. Visit markbeales.com.

Mauricio Velázquez de León Regular contributor to Lonely Planet guides on Mexico and *Saveur* magazine. He lives in the United States, thousands of miles from his favorite taqueria.

Nana Luckham One-time editor in London and UN press officer in New York, Nana since became a full-time travel writer and has hauled her backpack all over Africa to research guidebooks.

Paul Bloomfield Contributor to *The Times, Daily Telegraph*, *Wanderlust* and BBC Wildlife, Asia obsessive, man on a mission to find the perfect noodle soup.

Penny Watson Based in Hong Kong, Penny writes food and travel articles for newspapers, magazines, guidebooks and coffee table tomes. Some like it hot; Penny is one of them.

Phillip Tang Phillip writes about travel from his two loves, Asia and Latin America. He contributes to Lonely Planet's *Peru, Mexico, China, Japan*, and *Korea*. More words and pictures: phillptang.co.uk.

Piera Chen Travel addict, sometime poet, (co-)author of Lonely Planet's books on Hong Kong and China, Piera takes her rice with a baby-fistful of fresh chillies, finely chopped.

Rob Whyte Long-time resident of South Korea, contributor

to Lonely Planet books on Korean food and travel, intrepid countryside backpacker and Korean barbecue meat connoisseur.

Sarah Baxter Travel writer, Associate Editor of *Wanderlust* magazine and runner of marathons – to counterbalance the global eating.

Shawn Low Growing up in food-crazy Singapore endowed Shawn with a glutton complex and a tongue-of-steel that can withstand the fieriest of spices.

Simon Richmond Developed a taste for spicy ramen while living in Japan in the early 1990s. He's authored and contributed to scores of guidebooks for Lonely Planet, including *Japan*. www. simonrichmond.com

Stuart Butler Author of the Lonely Planet Ethiopia guide. He has written about things foodie for *Olive* magazine.

Tienlon Ho Enjoys travelling to places where she can eat innards and heads and no one cares, and has written about that and other things for Lonely Planet.

Virginia Jealous Has been travel writing for Lonely Planet since 1999. She's also a poet; her second collection, *Hidden World*, was published in 2013.

Will Gourlay Long-time Lonely Planet editor, and writer with a particular focus on Turkey. Often seen loitering near kebab stands.

INDEX

The World's Best Spicy Food

March 2017
Published by Lonely Planet Global Limited
CRN 554153

www.lonelyplanet.com

10 9 8 7 6 5 4 3 2 1

Printed in China
ISBN 978 1 78657 401 5
© Lonely Planet 2017
© Photographers as indicated 2017

Managing Director, Publishing Piers Pickard
Associate Publisher Robin Barton
Commissioning Editor Jessica Cole
Art Director Daniel Di Paolo
Layout Designer Hayley Warnham
Cover Illustrator David Doran
Editors Lucy Doncaster, Christina Webb
Pre-Press Production Nigel Longuet
Print Production Larissa Frost
Written by Abigail Blasi, Adam Karlin, Amy Karafin,
Anthony Ham, Austin Bush, Brett Atkinson,
Caroline Veldhuis, Emily Matchar, Ethan Gelber,
Isabella Noble, Jess Lee, Johanna Ashby,
Joe Bindloss, Joshua Samuel Brown, Karyn Noble,
Kate Thomas, Kate Whitfield, Lucy Corne,
Luke Waterson, Mark Beales, Mauricio Velázquez
de León, Nana Luckham, Paul Bloomfield,
Penny Watson, Phillip Tang, Piera Chen,
Rob Whyte, Sarah Baxter, Shawn Low,
Simon Richmond, Stuart Butler, Tienlon Ho,
Tom Parker Bowles, Virginia Jealous, Will Gourlay.

Lonely Planet Offices

AUSTRALIA
The Malt Store, Level 3, 551 Swanston St,
Carlton, Victoria 3053
T: 03 8379 8000

IRELAND
Unit E, Digital Court, The Digital Hub,
Rainsford St, Dublin 8

USA
124 Linden St, Oakland, CA 94607
T: 510 250 6400

UK
240 Blackfriars Rd, London SE1 8NW
T: 020 3771 5100

STAY IN TOUCH lonelyplanet.com/contact